Anatomy of Prison

Anatomy
of
PRISON

HUGH J. KLARE

HUTCHINSON OF LONDON

HUTCHINSON & CO. *(Publishers)* LTD
178–202 Great Portland Street, London, W.1

London Melbourne Sydney
Auckland Bombay Toronto
Johannesburg New York

★

First published 1960

*This book has been set in Baskerville type
face. It has been printed in Great Britain on
Antique Wove paper by Taylor Garnett
Evans & Co. Ltd., Watford, Herts, and
bound by them*

Contents

Illustrations

Author's Preface

PRISONS have existed for a very long time now, even though the aims of imprisonment have very greatly changed. However humanitarian they may have become in theory, in practice the men and women who are locked into an ordinary, local, maximum security jail—both prisoners and prison staff—are subjected to very considerable and sometimes damaging pressure.

The easiest way to relieve that pressure is to tear down the walls. Precisely this has, in fact, been done by the establishment of open prisons; and some critics have gone as far as to say that all maximum security prisons should be abolished.

I do not share that view. While I believe that some people are sent to prison who should never be sent there at all, I also think that treatment in a closed institution, given at the right moment, and lasting for the right time, may be the only chance which many offenders may get of growing out of anti-social attitudes.

This is, of course, begging many questions. But so far, penal policies have always been based on assumptions that have never been proved. There are good hopes that research may gradually enlighten us so that in future we shall have more factual knowledge about the effects of different sentences.

Meanwhile, let me make another one of my assumptions clear: the purpose of imprisonment should be the rehabilitation of offenders and the protection of society by preventing relapse into further crime. This view is not popular with some sections

9

of the community, whether they say so openly or not. But it is shared by many of the finest and most admirable members of the Prison Service, of all ranks, and their belief in the ultimate purpose of their work makes them the powerful influence for good that they are.

But they, too, are subject to pressure. This book is an attempt to analyse the nature of that pressure. It is a description, not of life and work in prison, but of the attitudes to life and to work which a large local prison may engender.

My primary purpose was to understand and to help others understand. I do not know how far I have succeeded. But I must ask the reader to remember that he is only looking at prison through my eyes. To emphasize this fact still further, I have made the narrative personal every now and then.

Behind the attempt to analyse and to understand, there was a secondary purpose. This was not so much to indicate means of relieving the pressure, as to suggest ways of controlling it deliberately, of using it fruitfully, of re-distributing it and guiding it into more constructive channels.

I am under no illusions that these suggestions would transform imprisonment. But I do believe they might go some way towards making the rehabilitative efforts of the men and women in the Prison Service more effective.

Finally, I must emphasize once more that it is in the nature of an account primarily concerned not with facts[1] and figures but with other people's feelings that it should be intuitive to some extent. Personal bias is bound to have crept in. What follows, therefore, is not the truth about prison but only the truth as I see it.

H. J. K.

---

[1] For a factual account of the administration of prisons, see Fox, L. W. *The English Prison and Borstal System.* Routledge & Kegan Paul. 1952.

Part I
A VIEW OF PRISON

1
The Concept

THE first time we had an ex-prisoner staying the night in our house, a friend asked us whether we were going to have the bed-linen fumigated. A little later, when we were going to a pantomime performed by prisoners, the same friend asked us whether the stage was separated from the auditorium by bars. No? Then what were we going to do if a prisoner suddenly turned and attacked us?

Dread of contamination and sometimes even physical fear of someone, not because he is, in fact, dirty or diseased, or dangerous, but simply because he is a convicted criminal, is quite a common reaction. I experienced it myself the first time I was alone in a room with a murderer. I well remember how reluctant I was to shake hands, and how unduly tense.

Yet on closer acquaintance, this man, who had killed another human being a long time ago, proved to be a deeply unhappy individual for whom it was not at all difficult to feel sympathy and concern.

This fear of contamination by the criminal goes back a long time, and has deep psychological roots. It does not even matter whether he is responsible for his crime or not. In *Sophoclean Tragedy* Professor C. M. Bowra makes this point clearly: 'Oedipus is not legally or morally guilty of murder or of incest, since he acted in ignorance. But he is something no less horrible: he is a polluted being, a man to be shunned as if he had literally some revolting and infectious plague.' And today, in spite of enlightened minority opinion, under the surface there is still the same irrational dread of pollution as well as the old desire to make the offender suffer.

It is not surprising, therefore, that the concept of prison includes in it ideas and meanings many of which inspire fear and most of which are deeply significant and dramatic. These meanings, however, vary considerably from person to person. To the average man prison is one thing, to the judge another, to the mother of a delinquent boy something else again. The victim of an offence, and his attacker, will usually look upon jail with very different eyes. And even amongst prisoners, there are considerable variations of feeling. To the middle-class first offender prison means inexorable exposure, ruin, social disgrace, utter degradation. To the habitual criminal it may perhaps mean a rather unpleasant professional risk which he deliberately takes; or if he is one of the many inadequate drifters who populate our prisons, it may mean relief from the demands of the world, a shelter where he can at least be sure of bread and board. To the man who does a long sentence it may seem like eternal bitterness, to the youngster who got off lightly it may be the beginning of a fresh start.

It is the image of prison which is evoked in the minds of the public at large, however, which is of the greatest significance, for this determines ultimately what sort of a place it is, or can become. It may, for example, affect readiness to spend money on suitable staff and buildings, or to tolerate new reforms. And in so far as these may succeed in cutting down the rate of relapse into crime, and thereby increase the protection of the public, the average man's picture of jail influences the effectiveness of our penal methods.

Perhaps the most common concept of prison is of a place of punishment where criminals are herded together and held in custody. Implicit in this is the idea of expulsion and banishment, age-old and linked to the fear of contamination. The high wall which separates offenders from the rest of mankind, and literally keeps them out of sight, serves also constantly to remind those within that they are in a different world. Prison is, in fact, a powerful psychological symbol. It is a place where people who do bad things—things which we may sometimes be tempted to do ourselves—are kept apart and held in check, just as we must keep apart and hold in check our bad thoughts.

The force of this symbol is shown by public reaction to a prisoner's escape. As a matter of sober fact, thousands of people walk the streets at this very moment who at some future date within the next twenty years are going to commit murder. One escaped prisoner does not seriously increase the danger to the public. Indeed, such serious danger as exists probably increases in proportion to the fierceness of the clamour which may drive the escaping prisoner to adopt desperate measures.

Significantly, an absconder from an open prison, where no one is held captive by force, will get little attention from the public. It is the man who breaks out from behind the walls who gets the headlines. He must be seen to be caught and locked up again, safely and securely, just as an errant bad thought must be locked away again. But meanwhile, there is a thrill to be had at the thought of the temporary break-out, just as there is at giving way momentarily to temptation. Yet the very same man whose escape made so many people hold their breath will evoke little interest when he is lawfully released a year later. Except that, perhaps, some newspaper may reward him handsomely so that the story of his getaway may be vicariously enjoyed again by its readers.

This often unacknowledged feeling that offenders should be suppressed like undesirable ideas colours the whole attitude of the public towards prison. It is mainly responsible for the very considerable emphasis on security which the penal administrator is forced to adopt, even though he knows that the interests of security and the interests of treatment and rehabilitation may be diametrically opposed. Any Home Secretary, told that if he instituted a particular régime, 5,000 prisoners would almost certainly become law-abiding citizens but 500 would almost certainly escape, is bound to hesitate: escaping prisoners are news, rehabilitated ones are not.

The number of really dangerous men in prison, in this country at any rate, is really quite small. Nevertheless, thousands of comparatively harmless minor offenders find themselves every year behind the same massive walls which surround the most aggressive and anti-social, and the same heavy steel doors clang shut behind them as they are locked into their cells. This may seem like using a sledgehammer to squash a fly, but it certainly corresponds to the picture the public has in mind of prison; a picture, too, of a world neatly divided into black and white. A man is a prisoner, therefore he must be bad, and a prison is a place where bad men are locked away.

This view accounts also for the exaggerated fears which are expressed wherever the Prison Commissioners try to open a new prison without bars. As soon as a site is chosen, voices of protest are raised all over the neighbourhood, and wives and children are declared to be in mortal danger. Yet if the Commissioners, having stoically weathered the storm, do succeed in opening the place, things change.

As prisoners are employed on local farms or in small factories, so it becomes clear not only that they are much like everyone else, but also that the neighbourhood may be able to play its part in the rehabilitative effort—a fact which will often occasion justifiable pride and result in a very different view of prison.

Such a fruitful co-operation between a prison and the surrounding community is still fairly rare, and depends on the comparative absence of natural and artificial barriers. But even in a maximum security prison, once representatives of the public do penetrate into jail, their concept of it is likely to undergo considerable change. Particularly is this so if they are allowed to come into personal contact with individual prisoners, as voluntary prison visitors do.

Newspapers reporting a trial will describe a burglar, a thief, or a sex offender. But once one of their readers becomes a prison visitor, he will quite probably not see burglars, thieves or sex offenders, he will see Joe Snooks who is in trouble. To such a reader prison becomes a place full of people like Joe, whose real difficulties will begin when they come out, who will have a hard time getting a job, whose future is dark and uncertain. He may be at one with the rest of the public in condemning their deeds, but it is not deeds that are locked up in prison but human beings, many of them with grave personal problems which they cannot solve by themselves, and for which they need help.

16

In practice, it is upon this view of prison that the policy of penal administrators in most civilized countries is based. By keeping before them the aims of reform and rehabilitation, they are considerably ahead of majority opinion—a fact which tends to be ignored by their progressive critics. To what extent these aims are actually being achieved, however, has yet to be adequately assessed. Perhaps it needs to be more clearly understood, too, that an improvement in prison conditions is not necessarily synonymous with rehabilitation, and that, so far from pampering prisoners, more effective rehabilitative measures may well make greater demands upon them than some present methods of treatment.

2
The Buildings

WHETHER he likes it or not, to the man who gets a long sentence prison is also his home. A temporary home, it is true, but nevertheless the place where, perhaps for years on end, he will sleep and eat, dream and wake, have his quarrels and reconciliations. To the staff, prison may not be home, but it is certainly the place where their whole working life is spent, and to some it is a good deal more than that: the scene of endless endeavour, occasional triumph and frequent frustration.

What, then, is it like, this place where people live in captivity, and work in physical and psychological isolation? What are the prison buildings like, and how important are they in determining the general atmosphere, and influencing the nature and degree of human contact and personal relations?

Most prisons in England were built during the last century, many of them a hundred years ago. From the outside, they look powerful, forbidding, desolate. If they were people, they would be huge, surly brutes, in threadbare clothes, with a look of fanatical puritanism in their eyes.

Inside, some of their lay-out has been influenced by the notions of Jeremy Bentham who was very much more interested in ideas than in people. Tall, gaunt blocks of brick and mortar, with reluctant windows, stretch out from a central point like spokes from the hub of a wheel. Administrative buildings may be, and workshops usually are, separate. Outside the surrounding wall, but often within its brooding shadow, there are the staff quarters.

Each cell-block has two, three or even four tiers of cells squeezed in orderly rows along both walls. The middle is left free and forms a tall and sombre tunnel which magnifies sound and entraps smell. Standing at the central point from which the various cell-blocks run outwards—radiate hardly seems the appropriate word—it is thus possible, with one shout, to reach the eardrums of every inmate of even a large prison. What is more to the point, by glancing in turn down each tunnel, it is possible to survey the whole of the prison from one spot. To provide which facility this peculiar structure was, of course, adopted.

Accepting for the moment that it really does serve the interests of security, what does it entail in terms of living and working? What sort of problems does it pose as far as rehabilitative efforts are concerned?

Perhaps the first thing to note is that as many as a thousand prisoners may have to live herded together in what is, in effect, one building. This results in a perturbing devaluation of human beings. If anyone doubts this, let him stand in the middle of one of these large old prisons at, say, nine o'clock in the evening. Let him stand, *alone*, in an island of silence, and feel the pressure. Let him listen to the place creak and buzz as the animals stir in their cages, so strongly locked, so securely barred, and let him reflect. . . .

As far as security and proper control is concerned, it can be argued that the structure of these big old prisons, as well as some of the administrative arrangements, is actually a hindrance rather than a help. Large groups of prisoners come together at various times of the day, particularly during exercise. Also, some of the big workshops may contain as many as a hundred prisoners at a time. But any large group of prisoners will contain a good proportion of unstable individuals, some of them tempestuous and explosive. It is, therefore, not surprising that the more serious disturbances in prisons have tended to start in the exercise yard or in a workshop. And it is self-evident that difficult persons are more easily handled in small rather than large groups.

At this point, I cannot refrain from quoting from an article in the *British Medical Journal* of 19 April, 1958. This describes the effect of a certain drug on mice, some of which were kept in smaller separate boxes, and others together in larger boxes. The excitement which the drug produced was much greater in the larger boxes, and observation showed that the behaviour of the mice 'becomes related to that of other mice in the box in such a way that mutual excitation of one mouse by another ultimately increases the excited behaviour of the group to tumultuous proportions.' Anyone who has been to a football match knows how quickly, and indeed tumultuously excitement is communicated. Mice evidently feel much the same as men.

But small groups do not only mean better and easier supervision and control than larger groups. They do not only mean that the most difficult offenders can be allocated and re-allocated to those groups where they are least disturbing; they also enable members of the staff to get to know prisoners, their characters and their problems as they could never get to know them if they had to deal with them only *en masse*. Finally, they make it possible deliberately to alter what might be termed the balance of personalities within the community of prisoners by judicious classification on the basis of the small group.

Here we touch upon the crux of the matter. The impact of prisoner on prisoner can be considerable, and though it may be useful and good, it may also be extremely harmful. A multitude of chance contacts, if they are of the wrong kind, may lead a man more deeply into crime. Moreover, such contacts, repeated again and again, gradually create a public opinion amongst prisoners. And public opinion is a very powerful thing, even though what is 'done' in the world outside may differ a lot from what is 'done' inside, and amongst prisoners. The system whereby large numbers of prisoners come together to some extent haphazardly for meals, recreation and work, allows opinions and pressures to be built up which can be so strong, and so negative, that much rehabilitative effort may come to nothing.

There is no doubt that the structure and lay-out of a prison building influences the prevailing atmosphere, and the morale of prisoners and staff. Indeed, the very size of the building is of importance. Though originally built to hold fewer, some of the old prisons in England and Wales house 900 or 1,000 men, and many house more than 500. Admittedly, this is small by American standards. There, there are some prisons holding as many as 4,000 prisoners and more—a veritable town, composed entirely of offenders, many of them serving very long sentences.

Here, the authorities seem to have come to the conclusion that 300 prisoners are about as many as ought to be housed in one institution. Certainly, that is the accommodation at the newly-built Everthorpe Hall, originally intended as a prison but now used as a borstal because of the increase in the number of borstal lads. Personally, I feel that even 300 is on the large side, and that the optimum number may not be much more than 150–200. With such a small number, the Governor has the all-important chance of getting to know all the prisoners in his charge personally—always provided their sentences are not too short.

Let me digress for a moment. It may not be generally known that roughly three out of every four prison sentences passed by the courts in England and Wales are for six months or less, and one out of two are for three months or less. One quarter of all the prison sentences are for five weeks or less, though by the time this book is published, the situation may have improved. Two Acts have recently been passed, one relating to civil prisoners and the other to first offenders. These may reduce the number of short sentences, and keep more people out of prison altogether.

From the point of view of training and rehabilitation, there is little to be said for sentences of a few days or even of a few weeks. It is hard to believe that anything positive could be achieved for what are often minor offenders, that could not be achieved equally well or better by dealing with them in some other way. (If they are in need of treatment and training, their sentence should be longer.) Yet the administrative arrangements for admitting, clothing, housing, feeding, and discharging again, a man or woman serving seven days are as time-consuming as for those serving seven years.

But to return to the buildings. Not all our prisons are built in the Pentonville style.[1] Some, like Wormwood Scrubs, have

---

[1] As described on p. 18.

separate cell-blocks which form usefully independent and self-contained units. Then there are small prisons, perhaps consisting of a single cell-block and a couple of Nissen huts. There are also open prisons which may simply be hutted camps or perhaps large converted houses somewhere in the country. And in the last few years, determined efforts have been made to improve the large old prisons with which the authorities appear to be saddled for many a year to come.[1] Much new lavatory accommodation has been installed and there is a lot of fresh paint in bright colours—light blues and ochres. But even with new dentures and bright ties, surly brutes are still surly brutes.

In any case, improvements of this type do not take us very far. These things are merely amenities, like film-shows on a Saturday night or a TV set in a recreation hut. They make captivity a little more bearable but they are not greatly relevant to the task of making a weak person stronger, a violent one better controlled, or a selfish one thoughtful. Nor do they prevent that accidental mixing and mingling which builds up the climate of opinion amongst prisoners—an opinion which is extraordinarily pervasive and is more often than not dominated by anti-social standards.

This same haphazard interplay of personalities within a large community of prisoners also makes it much more difficult for the staff to guide opinion along the right channels. And it is precisely by the almost insensible guidance of opinion, of feelings, and of attitudes that changes in outlook can best be brought about. You can *make* a man behave in a certain way while he is in prison, but it is much more difficult to make him *want* to behave in that way.

Yet is is only when a man genuinely wants to change that there is a real hope of rehabilitation. To create this want in him should be one of the principal aims of imprisonment.

In order to achieve it, I believe it is fundamental that the structure of a prison building should be the right one. Perhaps

---

[1] Since this was written, a Government White Paper has announced plans for a large new building programme. Inevitably this will take many years to complete. Meanwhile, a special building reseach unit has already undertaken useful studies, together with experts from the Ministry of Work, and has amongst other things evolved an entirely new type of cell, with a much larger window, at a much cheaper cost.

22

the ideal structure would be a prison for about 150–200 prisoners which is so arranged that small groups of, say, 12 prisoners could be kept living and working together, but separate from the other groups, except for such occasions as church services on Sundays or certain leisure activities in the evenings.

One could envisage that each section of 12 could have, for sleeping accommodation, a small dormitory and a few single cells; and that every section would have its own small workshop, and its own combined dining-*cum*-group discussion-*cum*-recreation room. Some of the most effective ways of influencing the climate of opinion in a group are keeping it small, selecting its members, helping them to discuss, and get insight into, their difficulties, and to accept their responsibilities.

These things can be done. Indeed, they are already being done, and with a good deal of success. for certain abnormal offenders at Wormwood Scrubs. They could be done for ordinary prisoners, though not overnight. For they presuppose, firstly, prison buildings constructed to cater for small groups, and secondly, more highly trained staff. And this, I believe, might be the pattern for the future.

Some people feel that prisons can never be anything other than necessary evils. I do not share this view at all. On the contrary, I believe that prison, rightly used, could sometimes be more effective in helping people to change and to grow than probation, with its comparatively fleeting contact with the offender.

That is not to say that, eventually, more people should be sent to prison. On the contrary, the more that can be kept out, the better. Nor do I suggest for one moment that prison could one day produce spectacular results and a negligible reconviction rate. Some people are probably incapable of change and growth, though age may bring about quiescence and a dying down of aggressive impulses. Others may perhaps be capable of responding, but we cannot help them for lack of knowledge.

However, I do think that there may be many who today leave prison, if not embittered, at least unchanged, and who could one day be helped. But the way ahead is not necessarily that of the traditional prison reformer: more work for prisoners,

23

better pay, and better physical conditions. These things are desirable, indeed essential, in present circumstances, and with the present buildings. But they are mere ameliorations, when what is wanted is a new and different approach, based on what little is known about the origins of criminal behaviour and checked by accurate information about the results achieved.

Part II
PRISON COMMUNITIES

Introductory Note

WHAT I have tried to say so far has been of a fairly general nature. I now propose to take the plunge and describe, in some detail, what it may feel like to be a governor, or a prison officer, or a prisoner.

Of course, I do not *know* what it is to work, or be held captive, in a prison. I can only guess, and I am bound to be wrong in many ways.

In that case, you may say, why attempt it at all? Because I believe that such an approach, by an outside observer, is not without value. However clumsily he may do it, and however blinded he may be by his own prejudices, if an observer genuinely attempts to put himself into the shoes of prisoners and staff in turn, instead of seeing the problems exclusively from one or the other point of view, a new dimension can be gained. And even if the picture lacks the sharpness and clarity which comes from certainty, at least it may dimly reveal a perspective which had hitherto been absent.

3
The Prisoners (1)

ASSUME for a moment that you have just been tried, and found guilty of a first offence for which you have been sentenced to eighteen months imprisonment at some provincial Court of Assize.

A Black Maria is taking you to a local prison, and inside that cage on wheels you have your first glimpse of those with whom you are going to live, in close proximity, for at least one whole year—assuming that you get your whole remission, which is one-third of your sentence.

You are still numb from the shock of the trial. Could this deceitful, worthless, unreliable creature whose misdeeds were pitilessly exposed and proved, point by point, really be you? Is it conceivable that you who have always wanted to do the right thing so much, have done so much wrong for so long? How could you have done it, what madness got into you? How will you ever face your wife again, your children, your friends?

It cannot be true, it is a terrible nightmare from the shame and humiliation of which you will wake up. And these creatures next to you, these burglars, thieves, swindlers and rapists, have you the slightest thing in common with them? Do you have to share your agony and degradation with these men?

It is too much. You cannot face it. And for the next few days, when you seem to sink deeper into the mire as you leave the world you know behind you, and enter the strange sub-world behind walls, it is as if your spirit had taken leave of your body, and watched it from afar, as you go through the required motions.

Something of this devastating shock, and the subsequent feeling of depersonalization, has been explained to me by many a first offender. And usually, such people have remained first offenders, despite the social consequences of their conviction, which can be considerable, and are often worse for first offenders than for recidivists. They are shattered by the abrupt rejection by a society which, so far, had accepted them. And with all their being, they strive for re-acceptance, however painful it is to start afresh, with a diminished status, and probably less income and a badly shaken self-confidence.

Statistics show that roughly four out of five first offenders do not offend again, no matter what sentence is imposed. Whatever their crime, and whatever their punishment, they have in common their trial, which rips away a mask and exposes their weakness and their failure to the public. I believe that those who succeed in re-establishing themselves also share precisely this strong desire to belong to a society whose goodwill they have only just lost but hope to win again. They do not regard themselves as criminals, and if they divide the world into 'we' and 'they', they are usually, though not always, on the side of the conforming majority.

Not so the habitual criminal. The 'they' in his world are all the law-abiding citizens, the respectable, the reliable, the people who read headlines but rarely make them, and those who regard the policeman on the beat as a harmless and friendly figure whom you ask the way if you are lost.

The habitual offender often knows no real 'we', only an 'I', for he tends to be lonely and friendless, unable to take a genuine interest in others. It is true that a discharged prisoner can often get spontaneous and generous help from the underworld. But such friendship is evanescent. There may be parties, laughter, excitement, but there is seldom anyone on whom the real criminal can rely. He is hardened to treachery (as are those around him) he is unstable, he never really trusts or is trusted. It is not surprising that he finds it practically impossible to establish a lasting relationship. His is a bleak world, and he walks through it, eyes moving from side to side, on the alert for a snatched chance, on guard against all. If he is very aggressive, he often believes himself to be hateful, and looks for opportunities to confirm this belief.

The law-abiding citizen is deterred from wrong-doing, not so much by fear of punishment, but by his conscience, and by his continuing need to be approved by his friends. The man who commits one offence, may still be dismayed by what he has done, and by the disapprobation of society. But the habitual offender usually takes this disapprobation for granted. Often his experience of life has been such that he has come to expect it, first from those who represent authority in childhood, such as parents and teachers, and later from those who represent it in adult life, employers, policemen, judges, and prison officials. In the end, he may lead a perpetual war against authority, and so far from being deterred by the prospect of punishment, he may unconsciously come to rely on it, indeed to look forward to it, as a means of reinforcing his convictions, and restoking the fires of his resentment.

It is remarkable how conservative many old lags and habitual criminals are. They want the old, well-known discipline and often dislike a modern approach such as the Norwich experiment.[1] In this, they are joined by some of the older prison officers, so that, occasionally, a prison may seem to be full of men who do not want to be rehabilitated, watched over by men who do not want to rehabilitate them. In such a situation, both sides know exactly where they are, everyone's behaviour is reasonably predictable, and each side's idea about the other is most satisfactorily confirmed. This self-perpetuating mechanism used to flourish fairly widely but is now beginning to disappear.

It must not be thought, however, that the distinction between first offender and recidivist is sharp. Any distinction which is based on a legal criterion, such as the fact of conviction, is in any case bound to be somewhat artificial. The man convicted for the first time may have committed dozens of other offences over many years, but may have been lucky in not

[1] A régime first introduced at Norwich Prison. This is an ordinary small local prison but the atmosphere approximates that of a training prison. Cell doors are kept unlocked all day and officers are encouraged to get to know the problems of the small groups of prisoners specifically in their charge.

having been caught. He may be a clever and unscrupulous crook with a twisted personality whereas the old lag next to him in the Black Maria may be a harmless petty thief, inadequate and dim-witted.

The Prisoners (2)

But back to your first days in prison. Nothing can help you over the feeling of desolation and helplessness which may sweep over you as you are first locked into a cell. The locking of that door, and the assumption behind it that from a harmless and perhaps even respected citizen you suddenly appear to have changed to someone so ferocious, so appallingly dangerous that it is necessary to keep you in a cage like a wild animal, is something that you must try to come to terms with, in the solitude of your cell. And during that first, and perhaps sleepless, night the loss of all that you have known of love and affection, friendship and security, may seem almost too poignant to be borne.

And yet everything does pass, and gradually you will find yourself less preoccupied with your own problems, and more able to take in something of your surroundings. Your fellow prisoners will come into focus, and may begin to matter more and more. With them you share your indignity, from them you may receive cruelty or kindness, and to them you may confide some of your hopes and fears. Almost without being aware of it, you take your place within the prisoner community.

There are various leading figures in such a community. One or two may simply be men with a ready wit, with the knack of getting a laugh out of a situation. But the more important leaders are also likely to be the more determined criminals. Any leader often symbolizes certain aspirations in the members of his group. This is true whether he is president of the local Chamber of Commerce or head of a gang of juvenile delinquents. The qualities of the group are reflected to some extent in the qualities of its leader.

And just as the abnormal, irresponsible, immature and criminal community of prisoners throws up leaders in whom these traits are strongly represented, so will the abnormal, irresponsible, immature and criminal leaders reinforce the tendencies which already exist in that community. This process of mutuality generates a public opinion with a strongly criminal flavour. The notion that prisoners infect each other has therefore a basis of truth even though the way in which the infection is spread is not always as it is imagined.

The antidote of the early prison reformers to this infection was solitary confinement, and this is still used a good deal in continental prison systems. Administrators in this country, however, have for a long time now disliked the idea of solitary confinement, and rightly. Deliberately to deprive someone of social contacts over a prolonged period is unwise as well as cruel. Many prisoners have difficulties in establishing and maintaining such contacts satisfactorily anyhow, and a régime of solitary confinement may do some real harm.

On the other hand, the kindly ideas which underlie eating 'in association', or talking in workshops, can have undesirable consequences which have perhaps been ignored a little too easily so far. And the concept that prisoner public opinion, instead of being allowed to develop as a negative force, could be used constructively and fruitfully, has not made much headway yet.

Some prisoners are actually called leaders. These are men who have been selected by the authorities and on whom are placed certain responsibilities.[1] These official leaders are seldom the same men as the unofficial leaders in a prisoner community, although it is not unknown for a particularly truculent prisoner with some following to be chosen as an official leader. Such a choice can have gratifying results if the man concerned feels that real trust and responsibility are given, provided he is capable of responding to such a situation.

In general, however, official and unofficial leaders are different sets of people, and the former cut comparatively little ice with prisoners. If a prisoner community is, as I believe, a sort of mirror-society, and its whole structure is anti-authoritarian and inclined away from the accepted, then the imposition of leaders who are acceptable to authority is unlikely to alter

[1] The system of leaders is in fact only used in a few prisons of a special type.

that structure. However useful it may be, it does no fundamental good and may even do some harm in that it may give an illusory impression of genuine 'inmate-participation'.

Take, for instance, the question of meetings between prison officials and leaders. Occasionally, quite important questions may be discussed at such meetings, and the Governor may alter his policy in the light of such joint consultation. The new policy may well be right. And yet the prisoners will often resent it.

I remember several ex-prisoners really haranguing me on this point. 'These men represent no one,' they declare. 'We do not tell them what we think. The Governor does not ask us what we think. But if he spends one hour with these chaps, he thinks he has got inmate participation.'

The situation is, I suppose, analogous to what would happen if an industrial concern started having joint consultation, not with shop stewards, but with foremen. The shop-stewards represent labour but the foremen are picked by the management. The foremen may even know better where the shoe really pinches than the shop-steward. But they will never be regarded as representative. Any decision to which they agree in such a meeting would be considered an imposed decision by the men. The purpose of joint consultation is, of course, precisely to avoid imposed decisions and to arrive at joint conclusions.

Genuine inmate-participation in prison would have to be with leaders chosen or elected by prisoners, and there would have to be a proper system of reporting back. Agreed agendas would have to be published in advance. Sub-committees could be set up for different wings or parts of the prison, for democracy always works best in small units. Consultation could be between sub-leaders and subordinate staff, and main leaders and superior staff. Some such system could well repay the time and trouble spent on it, as leaders learn to discuss grievances instead of giving vent to their feelings by aggressive behaviour, and as they explain, and possibly defend, joint decisions to fellow prisoners. Even if only at short intervals, and perhaps superficially, they would be working with the staff, instead of against them.

It must not be imagined, however, that any such system by

itself would seriously undermine the structure of a prisoner community. Quite a few of the real leaders would probably refuse to co-operate, for the very good reason that if they did, they might not retain their leadership.

What may secretly appeal to many law-abiding citizens the criminal admires openly. Why slog away at a dull job when you can live a life of adventure, of hunting and being hunted, of outsmarting the rich (who are insured, anyway), of shocking the Philistines, of literally playing cops and robbers? Is there not a thrill in the careless, exulting defiance of authority?

The deliberate flaunting of authority is, in fact, an important element in leadership within a prisoner community. To this may sometimes be added the ability to set up a kind of counter authority, so that every now and then a Governor and a rebellious leader, like heads of two opposing armies, wage open or undeclared warfare.

Characteristic amongst such leaders is the 'baron'. In its medieval sense, the title is not inept, with its flavour of might being right.

The baron operates in tobacco, or 'snout'. He knows that no one can earn more than a few shillings a week, which will not buy much tobacco. He also knows that heavy smokers, suddenly deprived of their normal supply and perhaps living under considerable stress, will give their right arm for more tobacco. In fact, heavy smokers in prison find themselves in the position of drug addicts, with the drug suddenly withdrawn. Tobacco can therefore be peddled at very profitable rates, and since a lot of people smoke at least reasonably heavily, and may feel the need for a friendly cigarette particularly strongly when there is so little else which brings comfort or ease, tobacco often becomes a kind of alternative to money with which goods and services can be obtained on the black market. From the baron's point of view, this unofficial currency has the advantage of never depreciating since it literally goes up in smoke, and demand always exceeds supply.

The first thing a baron does is to accumulate a supply of tobacco. He spends every penny he can earn on laying it in, and though he hardly ever succeeds, he may try hard to smuggle some in. But capital alone is not enough. For he depends for his profits not only on a usurious rate of interest but also on his ability to control a gang of 'runners'. These runners must themselves be able to collect the interest from customers and, if necessary, back their threats with force. That means the baron must be a strong personality, resourceful (for he is watched with envy by other prisoners, and with suspicion by the officers), ruthless, and a good organizer. He pays his runners out of profits, and supervises their activities with care.

If he is successful, he wields considerable power. He is boss of a gang, and he has half the prison beholden to him. With his profits, he buys such luxuries as are obtainable, and with his power he gets obedience. It may matter a lot more to the individual prisoner to be on the right side of the baron than to be on the right side of the staff. And to be the former may mean plotting and deceiving, lying and stealing.

The barons are powerful leaders whose influence is direct. There are others whose importance depends less on force and more on status. Prestige attaches to certain types of crimes, for example. Safe-breakers, mailbag-robbers, and daring wage-snatchers are much looked up to. In fact, such offences do require intelligence and skill in planning and organization. But the prudence and foresight shown in actually committing the crime often desert these men, once the job is done. It is almost as if the crime matters more than the enjoyment of its spoils—which shows that the main motive may not necessarily be money but the achievement of a spectacular act of defiance of society.

Notoriety itself is greatly valued. Many discharged prisoners carry with them newspaper cuttings of their crime and their trial, and one clever forger who came to see me kept a press-cuttings book just as an actor or an author might keep reviews.

Swindlers and confidence tricksters are not particularly highly regarded, unless their exploits are fabulous. They are often men whose sense of reality is greatly impaired. They live in a world of fantasy, of fiction in which they are always richer, more powerful, more important than they really are. This world is so much more real to them than the real world that they are able to project it most plausibly. But the prisoners know that 'con-men con themselves'.

34

Status also attaches to punishment. As Mark Benney has pointed out, your first prison sentence is your passport to the underworld, and a term at Dartmoor, or a flogging, is the criminal's D.S.O. or V.C. In a different way, the particular job to which you are assigned in prison may also have a special significance, and, because of the influence or the perks that go with it, helps to determine your place in the social scale.

Bottom of that scale are usually the sex offenders. For one thing, apart from their compulsion, let us say, to exhibit themselves to little girls, such men are often meek and, in the eyes of their fellow-prisoners, uncomfortably law-abiding. For another, although the direct cause of a man's imprisonment may be burglary, he may well suffer from some sexual maladjustment himself. And rather than face up to this particular truth, he may sometimes prefer to express disapproval of such matters.

A community of prisoners, then, is heavily stratified. A newcomer will be assessed, and placed into the correct social stratum. Like most people, he needs approval and esteem, and may try to get this from his fellow prisoners. He will get it much more easily if, at least in some respects, he conforms to their standards and values, and it would be a grave mistake to underrate the kind of pressure he may experience.

Women in Prison (3)

The situation in a prison for women is rather different. In general, women offenders are much more individualistic than men. There are no women gangs though a few girls may attach themselves to a gang of youths. Their loyalty, however, is usually less to the gang than to individuals in the gang.

It is the same in prison. There are friendships, sometimes highly emotional friendships. And there are many rather isolated women prisoners who do not form a close relationship with anyone. But there are few genuine leaders and there are few genuine followers though there are many passive and feckless individuals.

Certainly, their common fate as prisoners is a bond at times,

35

and colours their general attitude to the staff. But this bond never seems to be quite so firm as it is with the men—perhaps because of a certain competitiveness. There seem to be more rivals at Holloway than at Pentonville.

Although there are not quite the same negative forces at work, yet the atmosphere is basically no better than in a men's prison. This may be because there is probably a higher percentage of deeply disturbed and abnormal offenders.

By and large, women do not make criminals. For every one female prisoner, there are twenty men. This does not mean that women are necessarily more honest. They may be involved in dishonesty, they may know about the criminal activities of their men, they may connive at them, and occasionally even incite someone to commit an offence. But by and large, their role is passive. Hostile feelings do not often find direct physical expression.

The most typical form of feminine delinquency is prostitution (though, technically, only soliciting is an offence). The behaviour of prostitutes illustrates how a-social girls and women can express their feelings of hostility, which in boys and men might lead to some direct act of aggression like burglary or assault.

Prostitution is not a sex offence in the ordinary sense. A man who exposes himself does so in the hope of sexual satisfaction. The last thing that a girl who solicits has in mind is to obtain sexual satisfaction from her different clients.[1] What she wants, in the first instance, is money.

The money thus earned is probably considerably more than she could earn by working—just as a burglar, by one judicious evening's work every six months, can keep himself in idleness. And yet, it is often not the money itself which is the attraction —for no sooner is it obtained than it is thrown away again. It is the payment which is significant—a constant reassurance of being wanted, in the most elementary sense of the word. This reassurance may be badly needed, for most prostitutes come from homes in which there was bitterness and a lack of love.

Making the customer pay is important also in another

[1] See also Rolph, C. H. (ed.), *Women of the Streets*. Secker & Warburg. 1956.

36

sense. The girl who is drifting into promiscuity may seek something which she is seldom able to obtain from her partners —a secure and stable relationship. If she does not get it, it may be her fault as much as that of her partner, for she may not be able to sustain a lasting relationship. But if she cannot, the chances are once again that she did not find happiness and security in her own home.

Casual relationships are never satisfactory—and the more casual they are, the less satisfactory do they tend to become. Eventually, these disappointments lead to dislike of, and disgust for, men—which may sometimes have been latent already owing to an unhappy relationship with the girl's father.[1]

To drive a hard bargain with often loveless men, and to deprive them quite deliberately of the affection which some of them are looking for, becomes the aim of most established prostitutes. It is a game they cannot play for too long without damaging their own personalities further. But it is an outlet for their feelings of hostility—just as straightforward delinquency often is for boys and men.

Apart from a number of prostitutes, prison usually contains many elderly inadequate women, some of them alcoholics. There are also some who have committed small thefts all their lives; but there are few professional criminals, and there is no really organized crime by women. There is also no organized 'baroning', and whatever occasional small plots there may be hatched are usually quickly discovered because of the lack of loyalty of the plotters.

The impression remains that the personalities of many women prisoners, particularly amongst persistent offenders, are very abnormal. But they are abnormal individuals who are thrown together in jail without really forming groups, or constituting a community.

[1] See Glover, E. *The Psychopathology of Prostitution.* I.S.T.D. 1957.

4
The Prison Officers (1)

IF you are an artist, or a doctor, or a barrow boy, you are your own master. Not for you the need to accommodate yourself to the whims of superiors, as you must if you work in a factory, or an office, or if you join the Army. You do not have to co-operate and get on with your equals, while all the time you are also competing with them for promotion. Nor do you have to face your former workmates in order to establish a newly-acquired authority, knowing they knew you and your faults when you were equals.

These stresses and strains are part of the experience of the majority of people in any highly organized, industrialized society. They are quite severe, and sometimes people cannot meet them.

If you are a prison officer, however, there are additional conflicts to cope with. Top of the list is the nature of the job itself. Prisoners are difficult, resentful people, often unstable, sometimes dangerous. It is the job of the prison officer to guard them and keep them where they are. But it is also his job to help in their rehabilitation. The requirements of security, and the aims of treatment and reform, may well clash from time to time.

Thirty years ago, the job was clear-cut. Locking and unlocking cells. Marching men backwards and forwards. Counting heads. Keeping discipline. Watching, ready to quell any rebellion and, above all, to prevent any escapes.

It was clear-cut, but it was not elevating. Keepers in a zoo must also lock the animals into their cages, and prevent escapes. But they are allowed, indeed encouraged, to befriend the animals, and it is this, and not the daily task of cleaning the cages or preparing the food that gives them satisfaction.

Thirty years ago, prison officers were not allowed to talk to their charges. They were specifically forbidden to develop any sort of personal relationship with them. And to the prisoners, they must have seemed the embodiment of negative authority. They were the people who stopped them talking. They turned the key that locked their cell, they kept them captive, they said NO.

It would have been fairly intolerable for officers if all the rules had been observed at the time. They were not, and plenty of old lags will testify to extra-curricular kindness and thoughtfulness of some of the officers of former days. Nevertheless, the purely custodial duties and the tradition of impersonality did produce a sense of distance, an almost impassable barrier of feeling. Some officers tended almost unconsciously to look upon prisoners as virtually sub-human—and *vice versa*. Here were two armies of natural enemies; and this view of authority as an enemy must have confirmed many a recidivist in his hatred of law and order, and many an agent of law and order in his hatred of the recidivist.

The atmosphere of prison in those days must therefore sometimes have been tense. And yet this clear-cut division into black and white, into good and bad, must have given a certain sense of security, and even of satisfaction, to many officers. They knew exactly where they were. There were no half-tones, no compromises in their instructions. They had to keep discipline, and keep discipline they would.

But there is another aspect to this situation—unacknowledged but important. Taking the long view, the Prison Service was not particularly attractive as a career. True, it was secure and it was pensionable. But it did not take you overseas, as the fighting services did. It was not as well paid as the police, nor did it give you anything like the same opportunities for promotion. Taking the short view, regarded as a job of work to be done here and now, it meant long periods of boredom interspersed with occasional sharp bursts of danger. It implied being locked behind prison walls more or less for the rest of your working life. It brought comparatively little public approbation, and comparatively much criticism—triggered off by ex-prisoners and penal reformers on the one hand, and die-hard reactionaries on the other. Above all, it meant living with criminals.

And yet, the very fact of having bad people in your custody carries the implication that you must be good, otherwise you would not be in charge of them. Prison officers were not sadists, nor were they inhuman, thoughtless or unkind. But having been deprived of a good many satisfactions and of a more positive content in their work, at least they needed to feel good by contrast. And every time the Prison Commissioners, or a progressive Governor, or a penal reformer, appeared to take away a little badness from prisoners, it seemed to them as if a little goodness were being taken from themselves. Without reactionary intent, many of these decent men and women tended to feel that reforms would undermine their security.

And to some extent they were right. Not so much in the physical sense—though that is how many thought about it—but in the psychological sense. An officer who is in the lowest grade of a uniformed service, organized on military lines, who stays there for many years (until recently, it took an average of nineteen years to get the first promotion);[1] and who, as the recipient of orders from above has to salute, and defer to, so many for so long, may well feel that his status is bound up with his superiority over the prisoners in his charge. Raise the status of prisoners, diminish the social disapproval shown towards them, and you may make the officer feel uneasy and insecure.

Some worried officers believe that events are proving their fears right. The increasing humanity shown towards prisoners, the interest in their welfare, all the educational and rehabilitative efforts of the last thirty years have recently culminated in the Norwich experiment. According to this, officers are encouraged to get to know prisoners personally, to find out some of their problems and difficulties, and to pass their observations on to their superiors or to the Discharged Prisoners' Aid Committee.

[1] Owing to the war when the prison service was understaffed and recruitment was affected, promotion will be quicker for the next few years.

There is no question but that these developments are to be welcomed. Effective rehabilitative efforts are bound to concern themselves with the personal problems of prisoners, and, if nothing else, it would be a great waste of useful personnel if officers who are in constant touch with prisoners were not brought into these efforts, as already happens in borstals and training prisons. But there is another reason why the Norwich experiment is important. It is that the new duties may increasingly permit a positive relationship to develop between officers and prisoners, and that such rehabilitative work could lead to new satisfactions and to a new pride in the job to be done.

They could do these things but they do not necessarily do so. If the increased attention to the welfare of the prisoner implies a rise in his status, the rise in the status of officers is perhaps less evident. If the prison régime is far less repressive and much more permissive as far as the offender is concerned, the change that has occurred in the treatment of ordinary officers by their superiors may not always appear to them correspondingly great. Indeed, it may sometimes seem to them almost the other way round. Whereas in former days, a strict Governor would support, with rigid enforcement of rules and of discipline, a strict staff, nowadays a progressive Governor, by taking more interest in the prisoner, might at least seem to some officers to give the staff less support.

It is at this point that further progress in rehabilitation could falter. In so far as prison reform consists of administrative changes, it can be enforced from the top. But in so far as it consists of changes in attitude, it cannot be forced at all, but only encouraged to grow. And if the officer is really to change his role *vis-à-vis* the prisoner then the Governor should also change his role *vis-à-vis* the officer. And not only the Governor but all those who are superior to ordinary officers. Instead of only exacting obedience to orders, they should be prepared to consult, to seek co-operation. Instead of merely asking for discipline, they should give more guidance and advice. If the needs of the prisoners are to be increasingly considered, so should the needs of the officers.[1] Ultimately, this may mean a prison

[1] It is only fair to point out that this process is already well on the way in many borstals and some prisons.

service totally different in character and in structure from the authoritarian service we now know.

It is, of course, not possible to run before you can walk, and in any case, the purpose of this chapter is not to suggest how changes could be brought about but merely to analyse the feelings which probably exist amongst the prison officer community. That these feelings are not all entirely in favour of official policy can hardly be denied. When the Chairman of the Prison Officers' Association addressed the annual conference recently, some of what he said was in effect a criticism of the increased attention to the needs and the welfare of offenders. He went as far as to declare that:

'It is certain that, in the case of the persistent offender, the use of prisons and borstal institutions as a deterrent has almost completely disappeared',

and pointed out that:

'the experiments which have been tried out have tended to confuse the staffs, and it is with some justification that we ask: where are we going and what is expected of us?'

At about the same time, the Prison Officers' Association published a prize article in their monthly magazine, containing the following passages:

'Let it never be said, and in truth I am sure it never can be, that the officer in our prisons and institutions deprecates new steps in reform; on the contrary, generally speaking, he welcomes them with open arms. The facts are, however, that he is not prepared (and rightly so), to accept them at the expense of his own standards of life, and a reasonably acceptable status in the Service',

and elsewhere:

'The spirit of the Officer grade is treated too lightly by the hierarchy'.

Indeed, the article contained some much more strongly worded complaints, but these two passages seem to me to reflect quite fairly what some officers are feeling. It would be a mistake to underestimate these feelings. Most human beings have a need to be appreciated, to feel that they matter for their own sake, as individuals. Prison officers are no exception to this general rule, and in their situation it is not surprising that they feel somewhat frustrated.

For consider how hard it must sometimes be for them to make the effort to befriend prisoners. How often is a kindly gesture repulsed, how often is an understanding approach mistaken for weakness, how often is an officer provoked by a sullen and aggressive offender? And do not officers get attacked, and sometimes badly injured, by the very people they are supposed to help? Is it not asking a very great deal of officers to accept policy changes without a great deal of support?

I think it is. That is why, in their new role, they need a new treatment, a new consideration from their superiors, as well as guidance on how to cope with the inevitable conflicts which such a situation must bring with it.[1] Meanwhile, they are entitled to sympathy and respect from the public, and above all, from penal reformers. In fact, if penal reformers take it upon themselves to advocate changes which make greater demands upon the prison service, they incur a considerable moral obligation towards the members of that service. For outsiders to press for reforms, and then to condemn those who might have to carry them out as reactionary because they do not always receive such suggestions with marked relish, is not only thoughtless but unfair.

The Prison Officers (2)

The officers in a prison form a community just as prisoners do. Like prisoners, they wear a uniform and this is of psychological significance equally to wearer and beholder. The prisoners' uniform is usually fairly rough and badly cut, but

[1] It must be emphasized that in many prisons, the Governor and his Chief Officer are responsible for fostering a genuine spirit of mutual loyalty amongst all ranks of the staff. This, however, does not always mean that the new and changing problems of the subordinate staff are necessarily recognized or voiced. But once the problems begin to be recognized and voiced, the first steps towards their solution are already being taken.

even if it were not, so strong is the power of mental association that the most respectable of public figures, once one imagined them dressed in prison garb, could look remarkably criminal.

By contrast, the uniform of prison officers is well-cut and smart, emphasizing their superiority over the prisoners. (That is precisely the reason why many reformers want to get rid of it, and many officers are anxious to keep it.) And as with prisoners, the uniform underlines the common position and common interests of officers. On the surface, however, and probably at a deeper level also, the community of officers is more closely knit than that of prisoners.

There are many occasions when officers will act in concert spontaneously, and some when they must do so. The impulse to common action may come from different directions, for the officers are fighting on two different fronts, now facing the prisoners, now the authorities. Thus, if there is an attack by prisoners, officers will naturally rush to help each other. And if there is an order, let us say for a thorough search of prison premises, the officers will co-operate with each other in carrying out the wishes of their superiors. But another time they may carry a resolution criticizing policy, or pressing for a wage claim, in which case they co-operate against authority.

It is therefore not surprising that there are two different kinds of leaders amongst prison officers. The first of these is their superior officers. They lead by virtue of their rank, and their word, within defined limits, is law. But though their authority is great, they are not chosen leaders, nor do they reflect the culture and the norms of the officer community as nearly as do the leaders of the prisoner community.

The officers' most immediate superior is the Principal Officer. His position can be somewhat equivocal. He will remember his many years' service as an ordinary officer—as, indeed, will his new subordinates. And there may be times when, at heart, his loyalties are divided. Is he already completely part of the management, or is he still part of the workers? Does he feel with the officers when the Chief is in a bad mood, or does he identify himself with his superiors on stormy days?

44

No such doubt can normally exist about the Chief Officer. He is the head of the uniformed staff, and often the second most powerful man in authority. In the Governor's absence, he may 'act up', i.e. temporarily assume the Governor's function. Unless there is a basic difference in character or outlook, Governor and Chief Officer act as one, much as the Colonel and the Regimental Sergeant Major will act in unison in a regiment. This is not to say that differences in character or outlook between Governor and Chief do not occur. Nevertheless, fundamentally the Chief's position is not in doubt.

The slowness of promotion, particularly from basic grade officer to Principal Officer, is not only a source of considerable frustration but also not in the best interests of the service. It must be obvious, after a reasonable time, which officers are likely to make good principal officers. By the time nineteen years have passed, a good deal of initiative and originality may have passed also. Moreover, the Prison Officers' Association —the trade union of the officers—insists on a promotion procedure which gives a great deal of weight to seniority. This system is fair in the sense that it gives all officers an equal chance, but it is unfair to the younger officer of ability who ought to get on but cannot.

Unless he is good enough to be selected for direct promotion to Assistant Governor—now possible after two years' service[1]— the able young officer just has to stew in his own juice until his turn comes. It is perhaps not surprising that some of them feel rather frustrated, with men of possibly inferior calibre above them, simply by virtue of their seniority. They therefore tend to become leaders of another kind—officials of the Prison Officers' Association. And in a service which, because of the present promotion system, is perhaps a little more mediocre, more rigidly bound to tradition, less receptive to new ideas, and less adaptable than it need be, such leaders may sometimes seem rebellious, and infuse militancy into the Association.

They may, however, be truer leaders than promoted officers. Of course, they also have an easier task, for they can identify themselves wholeheartedly with the interests of the

[1] Provided he passes the long staff course. He has another chance after eight years' service and then only needs to pass a short staff course.

45

officers which a promoted leader cannot. The pattern of the relationship between the Prison Officers' Association and the Prison Commission which emerges from all this, is curious. The latter, as general policy makers, are progressive in their attitude to prisoners and prison reform, but as employers they may have to be conservative in their attitude to wage claims and other demands by prison officers. The latter, uneasy about their status *vis-à-vis* prisoners, are conservative in their attitude to prison reform, but militant, as trade unionists, in improving conditions for their members.

These differences in outlook are actually less acute than they seem. And when it comes to practical discussions and negotiations, yet another modifying factor is introduced. The Prison Commissioners are subject to Treasury control, and can only move within certain limitations. But they are also anxious to be good employers, and are strongly aware of their responsibilities towards their staff. So, within a conservative framework, dictated by their position as Civil Service employers, they try to be progressive.

The General Secretary of the Prison Officers' Association and his Executive are leaders of the local Association officials. These local officials can be more vocal but also more irresponsible than Headquarters, for they do not have to carry out the delicate task of negotiations. The negotiators themselves, however, though they must be active to keep the leadership, must also know how to give on one point in order to take another. Being closer to the centre than the local officials, they also understand the difficulties of the Prison Commissioners better. So that, within a militant framework, they must also practice moderation, as responsible union leaders.

This is not very different from the situation in industry generally. But one could wish it were. The worker in industry is ultimately concerned with objects, with things. The prison officer is concerned with human beings, with some of the most difficult human beings there are. The worker in industry is asked for more output. The prison officer is asked to develop a sympathetic understanding of those whom he sometimes fears and occasionally hates. He has to fight a great battle within himself, and one could wish that his superiors could spare him other fights. If only it were possible, in this one service, for negotiations about wages and conditions to be conducted direct with the Treasury!

It is not possible or practicable. But the further prison reform is pushed, the bigger are the psychological demands on officers. The recognition of this fact is likely to weigh more and more heavily with those in charge of the Prison Service.

5
Senior Staff

IT is hardly possible to call the senior staff in a prison a community. If it is a small local prison, there may only be one man —the Governor. And even in a large local prison, there probably is only the Deputy Governor and a couple of Assistant Governors in addition (specialist staff are dealt with in the next chapter). However, senior staff share certain duties and attitudes, and where the prison is special in some way—for example, where it is a large training establishment such as Wakefield—they do constitute a small group with certain common characteristics.

On the analogy with the armed services, senior staff are the commissioned officers. And as in the armed services, their clothes differ from those of their subordinates. But, significantly, that difference is not expressed in terms of a more splendid prison uniform but in the wearing of ordinary civilian clothes.

These civilian clothes are a manifestation of the sense of security which senior staff have regarding their social position in prison. They simply do not need to rely on a uniform to give them status in the eyes of the prisoners—towards many of whom they can also often afford to adopt something like the attitude of ordinary civilians. Moreover, civilian clothes help to underline the link with the world outside, and perhaps even to make relations with visitors to the prison easier and more informal.

It is incidentally noteworthy that in borstals staff of all grades wear civilian clothes. There, the status of the ordinary officer is usually more assured, if only because of the difference in age between himself and the youthful inmates. This often enables him to relax in his dealings with the lads in a way in which a young prison officer may find it difficult to relax when faced with older, or tougher, or better educated prisoners. It is precisely in such situations—i.e. in local or central prisons— that he needs most help from his own superiors.

The most junior amongst the senior staff is the Assistant Governor, Class II, or A.G.II. He is selected from amongst candidates from both inside and outside the service. So far, he is also the only member of the prison service to receive six months' training as a matter of course. Occasionally, he may already have had some social science training at one of the universities, but in any case he will go through some special training at the Staff College, Wakefield Prison, and Leeds University.

The newly appointed A.G.II has to come to terms with three sets of people. First, there is his relationship with his Governor. This is, of course, of cardinal importance to him. He is his chief, his teacher, often his friend, and always the man who can make or mar his first appointment and perhaps his whole future career in the service.

Then there are the officers. I have the impression that occasionally a young A.G.II makes the mistake of not putting quite enough thought and care into his relationship with officers. If things go a little wrong, this relationship can sometimes become rather strained. It is a point which the man appointed from outside needs to watch particularly.

The Prison Officers' Association is pledged to ensure that all appointments are ultimately made from within the service. The arguments in favour of this scheme are that it would improve the chances of promotion for officers, and that the better career prospects would attract more highly qualified candidates into the basic grade of the service, and thereby improve the general standard.

These arguments are important and deserve every possible sympathy. Nevertheless, I must make it clear that I am not in favour of the scheme. A competition which is open both to officers and to outsiders enables the Commissioners to cast their net very wide, and to make their selection from amongst

D   49 a large number of applicants. Also, some new blood at A.G.II level undoubtedly invigorates the service. At the same time, since basic grade officers are already eligible for selection and promotion straight to A.G.II, suitable young officers from within the service do have their chance. There is also a special scheme for older and more experienced officers to be promoted; and if they are already Chief Officers, they may be made A.G.Is straight away.

However, the fact remains that a newly-appointed A.G.II, especially if he is appointed from outside the service, must watch his relationship with the officers. Quite understandably, they do not like to see a comparatively young man, inexperienced in prison matters, over them—no matter what training and qualifications he may have. Tact and a genuine understanding of their feelings can straighten all this out, and by being on really good terms with officers, the new appointee will also be much more effective with prisoners.

Prisoners constitute, as it were, the third front. They are also the main front. Once a new A.G.II has covered his rear by being on the right terms both with his superiors and his subordinates, he can concentrate on the prisoners.

All the prisoners watch all the staff all the time, much more intently and closely than the staff watch the prisoners. After all, there are far fewer staff to watch. Weaknesses in the personality of individual staff members are invariably found out, and attempts are made, consciously or unconsciously, to exploit them.

On the other hand, there are the genuine problems of the prisoners. An A.G.II is in a particularly good position to get to know these, and how considerable and sometimes poignant they can be. He is also in a position to help and to influence at least some of the prisoners in his care. His attitude may make the difference between despair and hope, between angry rejection and painful acceptance.

All jobs in the prison service are worth while, but perhaps the job of an A.G.II is particularly worth while. He can do a good deal of personal rehabilitative work, and since he has been carefully selected and has had some training, he is well able to exploit this chance. The pitfalls are many, particularly serious being favouritism and other forms of the working out of his own inner problems on the prisoners. The rewards, in terms of worldly goods, are not large, though the Wynn-Parry Committee has recommended useful improvements. But there are many other satisfactions whose importance can never be estimated.

There are also many frustrations. The good A.G.II is always rather frustrated. Fully aware of the many problems that surround him, he is constantly asking for things, and often he cannot get them. What he does need from his superiors (to whom he may sometimes seem like a particularly demanding young cuckoo in the nest) is encouragement and patient understanding in large doses.

At the other end of the scale among the senior staff there is the Governor. His position is unique, and so are his responsibilities. No managing director of a munitions factory can have quite so much potentially explosive material about the place as he has. What he achieves, often against great odds, is seldom seen in perspective. But let there be an escape or some other trouble, and the spotlight is upon him with disconcerting rapidity.

Though he may not always see it in this light, the Governor's most important job is the reconciliation of conflicting interests. He has a duty towards his prisoners, and he has a duty towards his staff. Sometimes the interests of these two groups clash, and clash severely. To deal tactfully, wisely and justly with such situations, and to hold the prison together, often by sheer personality, is one of the most difficult and exacting jobs in the country. Not a few Governors in the English prison service do it supremely well. Such men—unknown though they may be to the public at large—are truly great.

It is relevant to mention at this point that all Assistant Commissioners and some Commissioners—i.e. the people who exercise central control over the prison system—are chosen from amongst Governors. This is both right and useful, and ensures that the men at the centre understand the day-to-day practical problems which Governors and staff have to face. It is also right that the main administrative jobs—Chairman, Secretary, and Establishments Officer of the Prison

Commission—should come from outside the prison service. It is precisely through such top appointments that broad new concepts can be introduced, and ideas cross-fertilized. This is not to say that broad new concepts do not come up from below. But a life-time in the service can make the most enthusiastic innovator stale, and the principle of appointing at least some top officials from outside the service is sound.

In an administrative system in which personnel and personalities count for so much, and in which there are infinite possibilities for tension and frustration, the post of Establishments Officer is particularly important. So much depends on the right handling of even quite trivial staff problems that the necessity for selecting the most suitable person as Establishments Officer cannot be sufficiently stressed. I wish he could also have the advice of a really first-rate social psychologist. If it pays to make such appointments in industry, it would surely pay twice over in a service which has to face so many greater and more complex problems in human relations.

6
Specialist Staff

THOUGH even small prisons have their Chaplain and at least a visiting M.O., only the larger prisons and training institutions have anything approaching a specialist staff. This may range from several doctors to social workers, from pharmacists to experts in vocational guidance, and from tutor organizers to psychologists. Complementary to these specialists, there are amongst the officer grade Trade Assistants and Instructors of various kinds in workshops, farms and so on.

The variety of specialists and tradesmen is very considerable, and each type has its own particular set of relationships, depending on function and social role. There are, however, two things which all specialist staff have in common.

One of these is their approach to prisoners. Specialists are not under the same obligation to enforce discipline as the rest of the staff. They may well have their own methods of dealing with difficult prisoners but safe custody and discipline is not their main responsibility. As a result, they are free to develop an easy and informal relationship with prisoners. This may be of an active kind such as a good Trade Instructor will build up with the men in his workshop, he leading and they following. Or it may be a passive, permissive, understanding relationship which a trained social worker knows how to foster, and which can lead to greater self-knowledge.

Such relationships are highly valued both by the prisoners and by the specialist staff. The personal satisfaction which the latter obtain in this may arise, of course, precisely from their positive social role—a good argument for ensuring that the role of the rest of the staff is never solely disciplinarian or custodial.

The other thing which specialists have in common is, as it were, the obverse side of this coin. Just because they do not have the burden of custodial and disciplinarian duties, and just because they do find it easier to develop a fruitful and constructive approach to prisoners, they may sometimes be regarded with a certain reserve by the rest of the staff. Discipline officers occasionally wonder whose 'side' the specialist takes—and in prison, it is only too easy to think in terms of sides. Or there may be some unconscious jealousy, particularly when two functions overlap a little—as, for example, in the case of an A.G.II and a social worker.

Both are concerned with rehabilitation. But the A.G.II must always remember that he is actually in charge of the prisoners, and indeed of the officers, who may be in his particular part of the prison. By contrast, the social worker can concentrate exclusively on case-work with individual prisoners in a way in which many an A.G.II might like to, but quite properly dare not.

Given this situation, it is surprising how comparatively little tension does develop in practice. When the Maxwell Committee first recommended that there should be full-time, trained social workers in all prisons, many an A.G.II was privately against it. Here were these case-workers, with all their training, coming in and putting his nose out of joint—or so he feared. In fact, the idea of a social worker turned out to be a good deal more sinister than the actual person. And in those prisons where there are both social workers and A.G.IIs, they work together amicably enough.

To some extent, the feeling of being odd man out, which a number of specialists have, may simply be due to the fact that some of the appointments are still rather new. The system has not had time to absorb them yet. This process of absorption needs constant watching and perhaps some speeding up.

If a prisoner breaks out in a rash, he is pushed on to the Doctor. If he is illiterate, that is the Tutor-Organizer's job. If he is a Baptist and wants to be received into the Church of England—off he goes to the Chaplain. Yet all the time he is

Joe Snooks, illegitimate, with three convictions for larceny, a hunch that he might do it again when he comes out, and an enormous chip on his shoulder. The Doctor, the Tutor-Organizer, the Chaplain and the Assistant Governor have really all got to deal with the same thing—the chip.

The official doctrine is that Governor and specialists work together as a team. This happens in some prisons, but in others there may be quite a gap between theory and practice. For practice means, not that the Doctor and the Governor slap each other on the back now and then, but that there are frequent if informal consultations on treatment—not on skin diseases or illiteracy, but on Joe Snooks, the whole man.

More often than not, however, everybody is far too busy doing something else. And how understandable that is when one looks at the list of reports the Doctor must prepare in time for the court next morning, or when one sees the Governor's schedule for the day. And yet—the reason that both of them have their job is Joe Snooks. And if we are really to establish in Joe, in the words of the prison rule, 'the will to lead a good and useful life on discharge, and to fit him to do so', then time will somehow have to be found for informal consultations. And not only with the specialist but also with the ordinary prison officer who can probably do as much to make or mar Joe's future.

Today, however, many specialists are still rather too isolated. It is a fate which they share with their colleagues in industry. But industry is concerned only with things. It ought not to happen in prison, which is concerned with people and their problems. The general integration of specialists into the prison service, however, is a long-term task of formidable complexity, both administratively and psychologically. Implied in it is a considerable reorganization of duties.

It would be wrong not to mention the executive and clerical staff of a prison. These men and women keep the administrative wheels going, and perform important tasks. But they are seldom in direct touch with prisoners, and do not have to face quite the same conflicts and difficulties. And since they are a little outside the main battlefield, no analysis of their situation has been attempted.

7

The Wynn-Parry Committee

I HOPE by now to have made clear my conviction that the Prison Service is going through a painful period of adjustment. Its members need the help and sympathy of an understanding and informed public and, above all, of those whose ideas may be responsible for some of the pain. They also need decent working conditions and pay—symbols of the esteem in which they are held by their employers, and by society at large.

The Departmental Committee which was set up in 1957 under the chairmanship of Mr. Justice Wynn-Parry, to inquire into remunerations and conditions of service of certain grades in the Prison Service, recognized this fully in their important Report, published in the autumn of 1958. Their most important positive recommendations relate to increases in pay, and particularly to increases in pay differentials, designed to make the service a more attractive career *(See facing page)*.

It will be seen that the biggest percentage increases are reserved for the lower grades in the service, to make these more attractive and perhaps also to serve as a substitute for greater job satisfaction—for the Norwich experiment cannot be expected to spread to all prisons overnight. But even the Norwich experiment, with its possibilities of playing an important part in rehabilitation, cannot by itself transform the role of the officer. For job satisfaction, as the Howard League pointed out to the Wynn-Parry Committee in a passage that ought by now to have a familiar ring,

RECOMMENDATIONS ON PAY IN ENGLAND AND WALES

Grade	Present Pay (annual)	Pay Recommended	% increase on maximum Pay
Director	£2,100 – £100 – £2,450	£2,750	12½%
Assistant Commissioner	£1,950 – £100 – £2,150	£2,450	14%
Governor, Class I	£2,050	£2,250	10%
Governor, Class II	£1,715 – £80 – £1,890	£1,800 – £50 – £2,000	5½%
Governor, Class III	£1,270 – 45 – £1,315 – £50 – £1,415 – £55 – £1,575	£1,450 – £50 – £1,650	5% (15% on minimum)
Assistant Governor Class I	£985 – £40 – £1,065 – £45 – £1,140	£1,200 – £40 – £1,350	18% (22% on minimum)
Assistant Governor Class II	£620 – £25 – £645 – £30 – £795 – £35 – £970	£800 – £30 – £1,100	12% (29% on minimum)
	(weekly)		
Chief Officer Class I	300/6 – 8/6 – 324/6	441/-	36% (46% on minimum)
Chief Officer Class II	276/6 – 7/6 – 291/-	402/6	38½% (46% on minimum)
Principal Officer	243/6 – 7/6 – 266/-	297/- – 9/6 – 345/-	30% (22% on minimum)
Officer	188/- – 6/- – 236/- 242/- after 10 years)	211/- – 7/6 – 268/-	13½% 13% on minimum

57

'is also measured in terms of responsibility, and in turn responsibility is measured in terms of trust, of the possibility of using personal judgment, and of the relationship to superiors. It is difficult to ask Officers to change their attitude to prisoners if their own superiors do not also change their attitude to them. Two things are required in this new situation: instead of superiors mainly exacting obedience to orders, they must be prepared to seek co-operation and to give a good deal of guidance and moral support. That is the first point. But they will not be able to give the right kind of support unless they have additional training—indeed, unless all ranks have additional training. That is the second point. It should gradually lead to the replacement of the traditional, old service discipline by a new professional discipline, akin to that of the trained social worker, based on confidence and some understanding of personality problems and man-management. The simple truth is that if personal responsibility is to be encouraged amongst prisoners, it must be even more encouraged amongst those who have to set them an example.

Training should, of course, be related to practice. Even in local prisons, matters should gradually be so arranged that there is adequate opportunity for discussion, consultation, and informal case-conferences at all levels. *Ad hoc* discussions and conferences guided by trained people are not only excellent in-service training methods in themselves, but they are a valuable means of improving communications—a vital matter in a large service which has to face such great tensions and difficulties, and has to work in such unnatural conditions. Some years ago, the Prison Commission set up Joint Consultative Committees, precisely in the hope of improving communication, of making their attitude, and that of the superior staff, known to their subordinates, and in turn learning the ideas and attitudes of the subordinate staff.

"One of the main functions of joint Consultation Committees," writes J. A. C. Brown, in *The Social Psychology of Industry*, "is to deal with such human matters as well as with the more technical difficulties which arise from time to time, but unless the atmosphere of the factory is good and a certain degree of mutual respect already exists, such Committees are likely to prove dreary sessions during which the workers' representatives rack their minds to produce all sorts of petty complaints but never get down to any of the more serious ones. . . . So far as co-operation or frank and mutual exchange of views is concerned, many of these Committees accomplish nothing. We have to face the paradoxical situation that the unhappy factory which most needs a competent Joint Consultation Committee is the very factory which can never make adequate use of it, whereas the factory with an atmosphere of friendliness and mutual trust which needs it less can always have adequate joint consultation."

Different prisons, no less than different factories, have joint Consultative Committees which vary greatly in their effectiveness. The more formal and authoritarian the tone of a particular establishment, the more difficult will it be suddenly to relax barriers at a Consultative Committee, only to re-erect them immediately afterwards. Nor is it necessarily very easy for the Prison Commission to judge the precise effectiveness of such Committees, for, in the words of Dr. Brown, "the desire to make a good impression may cause information passed up the line to be distorted. There is a tendency for management to be told that all is going according to plan (which, it is reasonably assumed, is what they want to hear)." When one remembers the poor promotion prospects which exist throughout the service, and then views these prospects against the background of an authoritarian service where position and status within the hierarchy matter so much, it would be surprising if Dr. Brown's findings were entirely inapplicable.'

The Wynn-Parry Committee tackled the thorny problem of promotion by recommending that after ten years' service officers could sit for a vocational examination, and if they passed this, should thereafter be entitled to the minimum pay of a Principal Officer. This recommendation may not be accepted in its precise form, but it is probable that the Prison Commission will agree that the passing of the examination should result in some pay increase—a kind of half-way house between basic grade Officer and Principal Officer, at least in terms of money.

Moreover, the big pay differentials suggested by the Committee may themselves be regarded as a kind of substitute for promotion. The elevations, when they do come, would be accompanied by such satisfactory increases in pay, and possibly prestige, that the period of waiting is made more worthwhile. Desirable though this is, it may also have some undesirable results. For the sense of inferiority which the basic grade Officer may experience, partly because he remains at the bottom of the service for so long, and partly because he may think that the status of the prisoner has improved in relation to himself—this feeling may be accentuated rather than diminished by the new pay structure.

Nor is this all. For most members of the Prison Service live in official quarters close to their work, and tend to form a separate community even outside prison—a community where rank continues to play its part, and may be reflected in the attitude of wives, and even of children, towards each other. This state of affairs—familiar in the Colonial and Armed Services—is seldom agreeable for the underdog. It may well be less so in the Prison Service just at the time when the basic grade officer is expected to show greater tolerance to often intolerable prisoners, and sufficient confidence in his own real worth not to mind the attitude of offenders who will constantly seek to prove him worthless.

The necessity for reassurance and for a genuine lift in status is patent. The first need in this connexion is for adequate training to give some understanding of their difficulties, and the ability to handle complex relations in the service. Such training must recognize and take into account the fact that though the man with low status may dislike his position, the man with relatively high status enjoys his, and may be reluctant to diminish the gulf. Nevertheless, training should be given not only high-status officials, for as the Howard League pointed out,

'all ranks need this, and perhaps none more than Principal Officers and Chief Officers. They are in closest contact with the Officers. They are also most strongly moulded by the authoritarian tradition of the service, and having been so moulded, then proceed to mould others. They are the nearest equivalent to what, in industry, would be foremen; and it may take a lot of training to broaden their outlook and enable them to become a source of real support to their subordinates.

Theirs is not an isolated case. Morton, in his *Introduction to Foremanship*, gives it as his opinion that failure to give praise is one of the outstanding drawbacks of British Industry, and Gordon Rattray Taylor notes that, at a foreman's meeting, it was discovered that eighteen foremen had reprimanded and only two praised someone in the course of the day. The art of management, at any level, consists in encouraging people to do their best, and not in stopping them from doing their worst.

As much would probably be learned by practice as by training. Once the habit of consultation and mutual support really gets a foothold, it is likely to grow. We referred earlier to case-conferences. This is the formal name of a procedure which can in fact be completely informal—a means of discussing the problems thrown up by the daily work situation, and in the understanding and management of prisoners. Indeed, the more Officers are encouraged to get to know individual prisoners and enter into their problems, the greater is the need for discussion and support.

Unless this is done, there may develop much informal communication between prisoners and Officers which is not fruitful, prison gossip which is without relevance or significance, but which can become undesirable. Prison Officers are sometimes unaware of the extent to which they may accept some of the standards and values of the prisoner community. What might be termed "auxiliary case-work" techniques must, therefore, be taught to every Prison Officer, and these techniques need constant reinforcement by discussion.

It is by informed discussion that a prison will get to know its real problems, and it is by making the fullest possible use, in consultations, of such experts as Medical Officers, Prison

Psychologists and Social Workers, that these discussions will become more profound, the task of rehabilitating the reclaimable more fully understood, and the members of the Prison Service more united in their aims.

Perhaps we may be allowed once more to quote an experiment from industry to illustrate the importance which we attach to discussion. It was carried out under the direction of the late Professor Kurt Lewin of the University of Iowa, in a factory in which output was dropping; there was a high labour turnover, and poor morale. The average rate of production had fallen from 75 units to 60 units per hour, paid by piece rate. The workers were asked to discuss the problems of production amongst themselves, and decide on a future target. The target suggested by the workers as a result of these meetings was 84 units per hour, to be attained within five days. Although the previous ceiling had never been higher than 75 units, the proposed goal was achieved, and was finally stabilized at 87 units per hour. In control experiments, it was found that asking, telling, ordering, or lecturing workers had no results—it was only when the group had adequately discussed the matter, and a group decision had been arrived at, that the goal was achieved.

The reasons why this is so are quite simple. People do not like to be ordered about like automata; they like to participate in a common task. They like to work for "us" rather than "them". Mutual discussion and common agreement lead to the acceptance of a common aim.'

The Wynn-Parry Committee made no recommendations on these matters, though they are likely to affect the quality of personnel recruited and retained in the Prison Service, and will certainly determine the pace at which advances can be made in the institutional treatment of offenders. Nevertheless, provided all these considerations are borne in mind by the Prison Commission, as they are likely to be, the advantages of the Report by the Committee should greatly outweigh the possible disadvantages. For its main recommendations would put the service on to an altogether new financial basis. They are public recognition of the debt which is owed to all those who serve in jail.

Part III
INDIVIDUALS IN JAIL

Introductory Note

In order to make absolutely certain that the identity of the three prisoners whose case-histories are given should not be established, names, dates, and other details have been jumbled. However, the cases are fairly typical of some of the persistent offenders who form the hard core of the prison population.

8

The Offenders

It was through his painting that I had got to know James. One day he came to the office and brought a head of Christ, curiously rigid, the colours harsh, but the paint splashed on with great intensity of feeling, and conveying an instant impression of suffering. He had, he explained, recently come out of prison, and while there, he had become very interested in painting, and wondered half-heartedly whether there was perhaps some sort of a job in which his painting might be useful.

'Not commercial art, of course. I only do religious painting.'

In fact, he only did heads of Christ, the same painting all over again, compulsively.

'I'll think about it. Meanwhile, tell me a bit about yourself.'

Telling about himself turned out to be what James had really come for. It was the first of many interviews. Afterwards I tried, in vain, to get one of the religious orders interested in his painting, or in James. Eventually, I got him a job as a clerk—but it did not last for more than a few days. By that time I had heard the different versions of his story, his mother's, his wife's, his teachers', his probation officer's, and quite a number by James himself. The essentials had emerged.

James was born twenty-seven years ago, an only son. His father had been a solicitor but at an early age had had a nervous breakdown. By the time James was born, his father was no longer a partner in the firm. Within the first ten years of his life, the family had moved eight times. Each time,

James's father had got a worse job, each time he had found it more difficult to cope, and his illness had got worse. Finally, he had been unable to work at all.

Throughout this period, James's mother had devoted herself to looking after her husband. His demands on her attention were constant and loud. James did not get much of a look-in. In fact, he was in the way. For as well as nursing a more and more difficult patient, she was absolutely determined to keep up appearances, whatever went on behind the lace curtains.

She was also determined to keep James up to the mark. He was a handsome child, and had better be a credit to her. But there were times when he would try her patience sorely. In a sudden rage, she would beat him—and then her mood would swing, she would be sorry, and hug her boy to her. For she realized how absorbed she was in her husband, and how absorbed her husband was in himself. It was really no wonder that James would get out of hand sometimes.

At his various schools, James acquired the reputation of being bright but unreliable. Like his father, he was very interested in religion and talked much of going into the Church. But doubts about his fitness grew more and more pronounced as it emerged that James could not stop lying. Instead of adapting himself to the reality of changing situations, he would adapt his fantasy world and remain the same himself.

Though endowed with considerable intelligence, he barely managed to matriculate, and was then called up. But his career as a soldier did not last long. He had rows with his hut mates and his sergeant, he could not accept discipline or responsibility, he ran away, and there was a tremendous scene when he was ordered to undergo a battle course. Three men had to hold him down as he screamed and kicked. Soon afterwards, he was discharged as psychologically unfit.

He got a job as a clerk in a large firm, and with the help of his uncle's car, he managed to cut quite a dash for a while. Good looking, he had plenty of girl friends whom he loved to show off. But none of his affairs lasted.

One day, he sold his uncle's car, and cleared out. He turned up in London and got a new job. His uncle accepted the loss of his car philosophically, but James never went near him again. He now met a girl to whom he proposed marriage. After a courtship of only three weeks, they were married. The day before the wedding, James lost his job.

With money from wedding presents they rented a furnished flat. Less than a month after the marriage, James stole some of the things belonging to the flat, sold them, and disappeared —but gave himself up to the police a couple of days later. The money he had received for the stolen objects went on an enormous eating spree, and to a prostitute whom he asked to beat him. He had been unable to consummate the marriage.

The court put him on probation, with a condition of undergoing some psychiatric treatment. But James lost three jobs in quick succession, would not attend his interviews, and soon committed another small theft—again giving himself up to the police. This time he was sent to prison for six months.

At first he settled down well in prison, but towards the end, he got very restless and several times provoked punishment, in the end losing all his remission. He did, however, greatly impress the art teacher, and it was then that he first started painting his heads of Christ.

By the time I met him, he had had two further sentences, and his life had fallen into a pattern. Prison, with settled behaviour at first, getting more and more disturbed towards the end—always provoking punishment. A short spell outside, a job, then running away; a minor theft, followed by overeating, and then a visit to a prostitute where he would ask to be beaten. After that, straight to the police, and the relief of prison and punishment again.

Once, I managed to get James admitted to a mental hospital, as a voluntary patient. Docile on entry, he resented the freedom he enjoyed there, and soon ran away. An electroencephalogram made at the hospital showed that the pattern of electrical impulses given out by his brain corresponded to that of a small child.

When last I heard of James, he was back in prison, this time serving rather a long sentence. He paints a lot and this helps to steady him. The other day, a visitor asked him if he came from a broken home. He said no, of course.

TOMMY

'I must get out of London,' Tommy said urgently. 'I'll never stay straight here.'

I did get him a job down in Gloucestershire. And for almost a year, I heard nothing more. Then one day, Tommy turned up again.

'A bloke I knew inside turned up. He blew the gaff and I had to clear out.'

This turned out to be only relatively true. A man who knew Tommy in prison did turn up—but his employers already knew that Tommy had been in prison. What really happened was that Tommy had met a girl whom he had dazzled with his adventures at sea. He had, he told her, been twice round the world. Knew South America like the back of his hand. Petty Officer, too. But last year, he had bought himself out of the Navy, and went to Gloucestershire. Of course, they would have him back any time.

He told others about his naval career too. But the man from jail had known Tommy for a long time and knew that the nearest he had ever been to a ship was when he was leaning over London Bridge, watching some barge being loaded.

Rather than face the collapse of his story, Tommy had cleared off.

There was, nevertheless, a grain of truth in this tale somewhere. For his father really had been in the Navy, and Tommy's stories about foreign parts were what he had often heard him tell. They had stuck in his mind ever since.

When Tommy was seven, his father died. There were two brothers and a sister, but Tommy was the youngest, and for a time, mother got very attached to him. Nothing was good enough for our Tom, and life looked very rosy. But when he was about fifteen, another man turned up and started courting mother. Eventually she married again, after endless rows with Tommy who was utterly opposed to this course.

But insult was to be heaped upon injury. For Tommy, who had found, and held down, a good job in a factory, was asked to put in a good word with the foreman for his new step-father. This he refused to do.

However, step-father got the job anyway. Three years went by, and things went from bad to worse at home. There were some changes made at the factory, and before he knew where he was, Tommy found himself working under his recently promoted rival.

This was too much. Without a word, Tommy put down his tools, and walked out of his job and his home. Due to be called up anyway, he volunteered for the Navy. But the Navy would not have him, having discovered some heart condition he knew nothing about.

Disconsolate, he drifted about, and in some café met a prostitute, no longer young, who decided to look after him. Through her and her friends, a new world opened up—a world divided into we and they, in which business girls and wide boys took advantage of mugs.

One day, some of Big Lena's friends asked Tommy whether he would like to be in on a 'job'. They had it all worked out and his part in it would be easy. If he didn't come in with them, why, it could only be because he was yellow.

Tommy went. The job came off all right, and the money was gleefully divided. Quite a lot of money. The next time they asked him, Tommy was keen to go. But this time, the job did not come off. And although the others got away, Tommy was caught.

He was sent to prison. When he came out, he swore he would go straight. But he could only get a poorly paid job, and soon some of the boys turned up, and persuaded him to come screwing with them again. Twice they succeeded, then Tommy was caught again.

When he came out of Pentonville, he looked for his prostitute. He could not find her. Meanwhile, he was contacted by some of his former friends. But he did not like the prospect of more Pentonville. Eventually, he came to us, wanting a job out of London.

When he came back from Gloucestershire, he decided that he could now risk London. And for more than nine months, he seemed to be all right, working quite hard, keeping in touch with us, getting through his money rather quickly, true, and

69

trying to borrow every now and then, but apparently staying out of trouble.

Then he got gradually depressed. He came drifting in and sat silent, dejected. One day he came in and said quietly:

'I'm going to give myself up.'

'What for?'

'A job I did. Months ago, it was. I never told you.'

And he did give himself up. He is back in prison now, planning to go into the Merchant Navy. I wrote to his mother for him, but she never replied.

BUSTY

Busty had a really bad reputation. I had heard of him long before I met him, for in one prison he had viciously attacked three officers at different times, and in another he had attempted to lead a riot. He was one of the few men who were hated and feared by prisoners and staff alike, and he gloried in it.

Busty was illegitimate, and so was his brother. One day, when Busty was three and his brother eleven, their mother walked out of the one room they all shared—and that was the last they ever saw of her. She had disappeared from time to time before but she had always returned.

The boys, used to turning to neighbours in such emergencies, thought she was bound to come back again. When one day after another went by, however, and still the mother did not return, the neighbours did not content themselves with grumbling. An N.S.P.C.C. inspector visiting the area was informed, and through him the police. Busty's mother could not be traced anywhere and eventually the two boys were found a foster home.

This proved to be a good move, for the family was a happy one and both boys seemed to settle down for a while. Busty began to show a marked attachment to his brother and things went far better than anyone had dared to hope. Then suddenly the father died, the boys had to be taken away again, and it proved impossible to place both of them together with another foster family.

This turned out to be the beginning of the end. Neither of the boys could get used to his new home. Both ran away, and then to crown everything, the older brother got himself into trouble with the police, and was sent to an Approved School. When he learnt of this, Busty became quite unmanageable and soon he, too, was in an Approved School. This was the start of a long career in penal institutions, marked by increasing hostility towards those in charge, and a fresh access of bitterness after the news was received of his brother's death at the age of twenty-four, killed in Italy.

Viewed in perspective, Busty's life was one long endeavour to prove to himself that 'they' were nasty, cruel, horrible, and in league with each other to do Busty down. Whenever he could, he provoked punishment, and the more he was punished, the more aggressive and hostile he got. Suspicious of kindness and sympathy, he found it difficult to accept friendship even from fellow prisoners—a blessing for the authorities, for it meant that he had virtually no following when he attempted to start some organized trouble.

I got to know him because he burst into the office one day, quivering with rage at our activities—or rather, lack of activities. Big, burly, strong as a bull, with hot blue eyes, he seemed likely to go off like a time bomb. After what was probably a fairly short time but seemed interminable, I managed to get him quietened down a little and talking about himself and his grievances.

Busty was not without occasional flashes of insight. Several times, for example, he said musingly that something seemed to drive him on to acts of aggression—in other words, he realized that the source of hostility really lay within himself, and not in others as he so often reiterated. He also described the definite sense of relief he obtained from the act of violence itself—smashing his fist into an officer's face—and from the punishment that followed. He had been flogged, was proud of it, and eager to show the marks on his back which he wore like medals.

After every incident, he would be put into a punishment cell, in solitary confinement, and he positively enjoyed these spells cut off from everyone else. People, he explained, really fell into two categories—those he disliked, and those he hated; and it almost seemed as though he was far more attracted by the latter than the former.

He described a moment of glory when he was in the Governor's office, after a long spell of defiance. No one else was in the room, just he and the Governor, and there ensued a brief battle of wills between them. 'That Governor,' said Busty, 'is a real b——, I hate his rotten guts, but one thing you got to give him: he's not yellow, he's a proper man.'

I asked Busty what he thought of himself. 'I'm the biggest b—— of them all, and I'm a real trouble-maker,' he said fiercely. His world was all black, all badness. He saw himself as someone hateful, and therefore to be hated, and the important others—judges, governors, cops and screws—all had to be provoked into the familiar attitudes of scorn and anger, thereby confirming Busty's inner picture of himself. Busty against the world, and the world against Busty, that was how it had always been, and that, if he had anything to do with it, was how it was going to stay.

9
The Officer

TOMMY, undepressed, is what officers are mostly faced with
in local prisons. He does not present any great problem, in
terms of getting him to conform to the present pattern of
prison life. And if an effort is made to establish contact, he is
open to influence—perhaps too open. As far as Tommy is
concerned, most officers would probably have no hesitation
in applying the Norwich system or better, and some
will do, whether the system has been officially introduced or
not.

It is, in fact, remarkable how convinced many officers are
about the tremendous importance and rightness of the reforma-
tive aspect of their work. In them, this conviction is usually an
extension of an already existing attitude, unconnected with
official policy, and finds expression in many simple acts of
kindliness. Quite often, their interest in the general implica-
tions of this aspect of their work will lead them to seek guidance
and training through attendance at lectures and summer
schools on the problems of delinquency and the treatment of
offenders.

Not all officers share this attitude, however. Nor can they
be forced to change their opinion, whatever the official policy
is. Indeed, such policy may genuinely seem unacceptable and
even dangerous to them because of the authoritarian structure
of their character. Their difficulties were expressed in another
slightly tongue-in-cheek prize article in the *Prison Officers'
Magazine* of November 1958:—

'If you are interested in advancement in the Prison Service you must make your choice between two pitiable alternatives. Either you will read the prescribed books and hold the prescribed opinions, or you will pay lip service to ideals which you do not share and keep your true opinions to yourself. Either way demands a surrender of self-respect which many of your colleagues . . . find too high a price to pay for promotion.'

It would be a mistake to take this article too seriously, but it would be equally wrong to write off this particular passage, and the note of sincerity it strikes, as expressing only the attitude of a small and dissatisfied minority. It was followed a month afterwards by a signed letter which was almost a *cri-de-coeur*:

'My hearty congratulations to the writer of the prize article (November). Surely this must be the prize article of the year? Could have been called quite easily "This Is Your Life".

All joking aside, let us be frank and admit that we Prison Officers are the only ones who know perfectly well that [the author] is quite right. If his article had been offered to the National Press they would have considered it as a leg-pull, an untruth, and would not have printed it.

Good gracious, no. The public, the taxpayers mustn't know the truth. . . .'

I believe there may be several reasons why officers feel like this. But the most important must lie in their own personality for how, otherwise, is it possible for two officers in the same prison to express diametrically opposed views on the purpose of prison and the nature of the offenders? What might be called the 'accepting' view was well expressed to a journalist writing recently in the *Sunday Times* (November 1958):

'You've got to trust [prisoners], otherwise you get nowhere. . . . Now that we're able to talk more freely with them, it's a great thing to know that something you say might help one of these chaps to improve himself. They're no angels, but in eighteen years I haven't met one who's all bad.'

The opposite or 'rejecting' view is hardened by the occasional presence of a James and a Busty, and by the never-ending trickle of near-defectives and incontinents who require limitless patience in their handling. The future development of classification will have to take account of the need for a balancing of personalities amongst prisoners, so that the staff is not too hard pressed at any one establishment.

This leads straight to the final point which is that there are always more 'accepting' officers at open and training institutions than at local maximum security prisons. In the latter, prisoners, officers, the type and structure of the building, and the degree of social control which is attempted, all interact upon each other to produce a much larger number of officers of the 'rejecting' type.

To Governors and Commissioners anxious to press on with reforms, these officers may sometimes seem maddeningly stubborn and wrong headed. Yet they are the very men who most need support from their own superiors, for the coming changes in attitude represent a threat to their most deeply held convictions. But there is an obvious lesson for selecting future personnel here—a lesson which should not be disregarded if we are to move towards a general democratization of prison régime.

10
The Social Worker

THERE are two types of trained social workers in English prisons—those who are now being appointed to prepare prisoners for discharge, and psychiatric social workers attached to psychiatric units. The latter are the more highly trained but both will tend to look at present behaviour in terms of the forces of the past which have shaped character and personality. Both may have to concern themselves with diagnosis and with treatment.

The social workers concerned with preparations for after-care—misnamed Welfare Officers by the Maxwell Committee on After-Care[1]—must be able to make a realistic assessment of a prisoner's personality in order to have a sound basis on which to make plans for life and work after release; plans which should be made with the prisoner and not merely for him.

In theory, treatment and after-care should be a continuous process. In practice it is not, and the difficulties in the way of making it so are formidable. For both prisoners and staff tend to regard life in prison and life outside as two quite different, almost unconnected things—the rules of the game are just not written by the same hand. There is, therefore, all the more reason for the social worker to attempt to bridge the gap.

He could do this by advising the prison staff about suitable work and training, perhaps including attendance at certain classes. The available alternatives are few enough in a local

[1] See Chapter 22.

prison, and the degree of difference which they could make is probably minute. More important, however, is the possibility which this might give of informal discussions with officers about the personality of the prisoner, his background, the type of problem that awaits him on release, the difficulties he may meet as a result of his personality, and what could be done in terms of personal relationship and attitude during his sentence to help him to meet these.

The other method by which the social worker can help to prepare him for release is by intensive case-work. By this I mean a series of interviews in which the prisoner is gradually helped to gain insight and to work through certain difficulties. This presupposes training of a high order on the part of the social worker. It also presupposes a selection of, and concentration on, quite a small number of prisoners who might benefit, rather than a more casual contact with a large and unselected number of offenders. Such selected case-work would probably be the most worth-while thing that could be attempted in an ordinary local prison at the present time.

Whatever the social worker does, he must be aware that, since he is not part of the discipline staff, his relationship with the prisoner is easier and more relaxed than that of an officer. This will be particularly so when case-work at a deeper level is attempted, for nothing could be in greater contrast to the impersonal grinding of the wheels of a large institution than the intimate and intensely personal *rapport* which is established between case-worker and client.

The social worker must be aware that his special relationship with prisoners may produce resentment and even jealousy amongst officers, and that the techniques which he uses may epitomize that permissive approach which a good many of the discipline staff genuinely fear as a threat to their security.

This is another reason why he should be encouraged to consult closely with officers. By a serious exchange of information on the personality and behaviour of individual prisoners, understanding and confidence could be built up between social worker and discipline staff. And as it is being built up, so the fears and anxieties of officers could be expressed. It cannot be emphasized too much how important it is to create

77

possibilities for the expression of these emotions, for, unexpressed, they will form the basis of resistance to change.

It could well be that, in this way, social workers could reduce tension and hostility between prisoners and staff. Such a healing influence would be in the highest tradition of the profession. And if the load of resentment can be lightened, at the very least it would represent a gain for the institution. But of course it is not the function of a prison simply to become an institution in which there is order and even a reasonable amount of content. The task is far more difficult and challenging. But in the search for rehabilitative forces, it may be that there are means of harnessing for more constructive purposes the energy freed from the bondage of negative emotions.

The psychiatric social worker may be still further removed from the discipline staff in that his (or her) work is centred on the psychiatric unit probably situated in the hospital. The matter is not helped by the general confusion of ideas which exists about the role of psychiatric treatment and the kind of persons selected to undergo it, and derisively referred to as 'nut-cases'. The fact remains that 'nut-cases' will contain a high proportion of those who are capable of responding to treatment whereas amongst the other prisoners there will be many whose abnormalities of character are so severe that they would not be considered for it.

The fact that these confusions exist and are perpetuated, is yet another reason why the psychiatric social worker, too, should seek as much contact with the discipline staff as possible.

11

The Chaplain

Not all Chaplains have welcomed the gradual development of social work in prison. Education and welfare used to be the exclusive preserve of the Church and Chaplains would often use these as a way of making contact with prisoners and, from this point of vantage, seek to reach or awaken religious feelings. Moreover, some Chaplains did—and do—consider it part of their Christian duty to have concern for the whole man and not just for his soul. But though even today, they still deal with such matters as the selection of prison visitors, and will usually sit on Discharge Boards, the tendency is for social work to be concentrated increasingly in secular hands.

This development is inevitable as social work becomes more specialized, takes up more time, and requires professional training. Current thinking, in this country at any rate, makes a fairly sharp distinction between where case-work ends and pastoral work begins.

I feel particularly ill qualified to voice an opinion on these matters but I should have thought that, just as it is unwise to make a firm division between the body and the mind, so it may be wrong to divide emotions from spirit. I do not think that Chaplains should do case-work but I do feel that it might be helpful for them to receive a thorough grounding in psychology, and particularly in the psychology of delinquent behaviour.

There seem to be a few rare and saintly people whose personality and belief is such that they make a direct and sometimes lasting impact on many of those who lie in jail. But not all Chaplains have this quality. At the same time, a considerable number of recidivist prisoners are emotionally so shallow that to minister to their spiritual needs, to evoke some genuine response, must be heartbreakingly difficult. It may be that psychological training might make this task a little easier.

Another possible difficulty which faces Chaplains is that, by being part and parcel of the prison, they may become identified with it in the minds of the prisoners. This can be avoided, and often is, but what Sir Lionel Fox calls 'that spiritual zest, that freshness of approach', is quite essential and must be preserved. Priests of denominations other than the Church of England may perhaps have an easier task in this respect since they come in to visit from outside. They are able to retain a certain aloofness from the day-to-day routine of prison which may be more difficult for a resident Chaplain. Nevertheless, I believe it is right to have resident Chaplains where possible so that they can be at hand whenever needed, and the impression which I have is that some of the finest pastoral work is done by apparently casual cell visits.

There are special times when such cell visits may be particularly rewarding. For example, there may come a point where the offender has gained sufficient insight to recognize and deplore—in his heart, and not only by fine phrases—the injury which he has done. This can be a truly terrible moment, especially for those who have done serious injury or who have committed murder. It is when true repentance begins that spiritual help and consolation is of greatest importance for all those who have any religious feelings at all. And in parenthesis, it might be pointed out to those who are opposed to case-work or a psychoanalytical approach on the grounds that it takes away personal responsibility, that the only chance of gaining insight (and thus of accepting personal responsibility) which some seemingly conscienceless recidivists have, may be the use of precisely this approach. Which seems to me one more reason why Chaplains, or Visiting Ministers, should have some understanding of it.

Maximum security prison, Wandsworth

Open prison, Falfield

Cells at Wandsworth

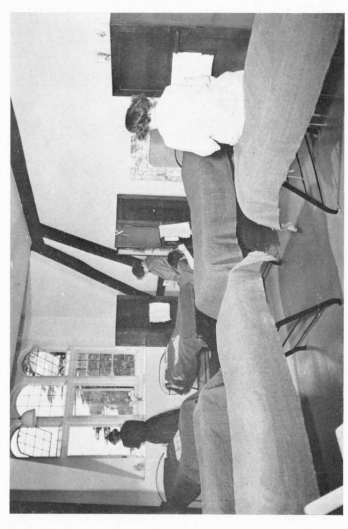

Dormitory at open prison for women, Hill Hall

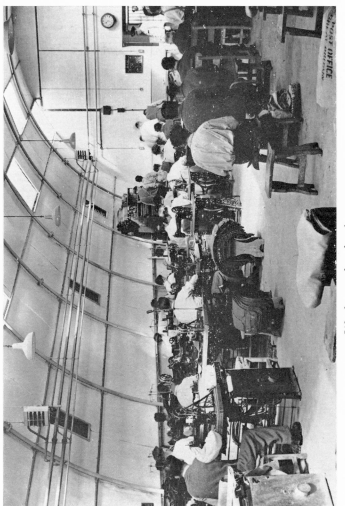

Work at a local prison

Art at a regional prison

Last glimpse of outside

First reunion

12
The Medical Officer

I SUPPOSE that one of the attractions in choosing medicine as a career is the chance it gives, not only of helping those who are sick, but of developing a good doctor-patient relationship. I believe this relationship is just as important to the doctor as it is to the patient. The confidence and trust which is reposed in him, the gratitude which patients feel and often spontaneously express—these must be some of the greatest satisfactions in the work of a medical practitioner.

It is true that in the relationship between a doctor and his patient, the doctor has psychologically the upper hand. For it is first of all the patient who wants something, and something that is of immediate and intimate concern to his health and well-being. In turn, the doctor is usually able to give something, whether it is medicine or reassurance. And it has been well said that the best medicine of all is the doctor himself, the hope and the faith which he can give and which may contribute more to recovery than any bottle or pills.

This hope and faith depends a good deal on the doctor's own personality, but I cannot help feeling that it also depends a little on the patient's ability to choose freely the doctor he wants; and even (this at the risk of being accused as a thorough reactionary) to pay him for his services which are valued in every sense of the word.

A prisoner cannot do any of this. He cannot choose his prison, his Governor or his doctor—once the sentence is passed, they are more or less Acts of God, as far as he is concerned. In the doctor's case, the same is true of the prisoner, and a thoroughly unsatisfactory patient he can make, too—partly because of the kind of person he is, and partly because of the circumstances in which he finds himself.

There is, in many recidivist prisoners, a sense of having been let down—as, indeed, they may have been, in childhood. This leads to a feeling that society owes them something, to an attitude that is continually demanding, like that of a small child. Prison tends to reinforce this attitude, through the dependence that it breeds, and through resentment at the attempt of total social control—again attributes of childhood.

In these circumstances, the doctor becomes a specially significant figure. He is not part of the custodial staff—and since he is not one of the 'no-sayers', the assumption is that he ought to be a 'yes-sayer'. Moreover, it is not as if he were just a social worker who, as everyone knows, does not wield any real power. On the contrary, the doctor wields considerable power—his veto can, for example, stop punishment.

Above all, however, the doctor is a health-giver or health-restorer—a maternal figure. And if Mum over-protected the prisoner in childhood, and the doctor now does not, then he is a sore disappointment. On the other hand, if Mum was rejecting, then the chances are that the doctor, in turn, may be rejected.

One of the figures who symbolizes this curious doctor-patient relationship is the 'lead-swinger'. But in a local prison, there is in fact precious little lead to swing. Work is so scarce that there is no point in getting out of it.

In a general way, lead swinging is probably evidence of low morale. In a particular case, it may be one of quite a number of different things: an attempt to gain sympathy, a desire to score off the discipline staff, an effort at evading reprisals by a fellow prisoner, some sort of a testing-out of the doctor, or perhaps simply an endeavour to prove that the prisoner is really much cleverer than that old fool of a quack.

What is the doctor to do? Once he has diagnosed lead-swinging, he has only diagnosed the symptom, not the cause. Patient and tactful examination may well reveal the latter—and often remove it, too, for extra personal attention will put many things right, with prisoners just as with children. Even the prisoner who is trying to be clever may half hope to fail.

Yet extra attention may be the one thing the doctor cannot afford. Nowadays, the writing of reports for the courts, sometimes in most difficult circumstances, puts a rapidly increasing burden on Prison Medical Officers. The eventual development of Remand and Observation Centres with their own diagnostic staff for the preparation of Court reports, should restore to the doctor in prison some of the time he needs. Meanwhile, he has to ration it, and by so doing risk yet another negative response.

The surprising thing is not that a few doctors may possibly allow their disappointment to colour their attitude a little but that so many remain strongly dedicated and idealistic, in spite of these and other difficulties. There are men in the Prison Medical Service who, in my opinion, are quite outstanding both as doctors and as human beings. I know that they find their work immensely worthwhile, not through any rewarding relationships, but through the satisfaction which is obtained by doing their best for difficult patients, and perhaps above all by being able to help stunted personalities to grow and develop.

For the Medical Officer has to deal both with physical and with psychological disorders. One of my friends thought this a disadvantage, holding that those doctors who were interested in general practice might not like psychiatric work, and those who were interested in psychiatric work might not care for general practice.

I believe, on the contrary, that if only they realized the full potential of it, many young doctors would be attracted to work of such an unusually challenging and broad nature. We have gone on long enough treating the body and the mind in separate compartments. No one is going to deny that these two are part and parcel of the same entity, that they interact, and that disorders in one may produce disorders in the other. The casualty patient admitted in a delusional state may be a schizophrenic, or he may be a diabetic suffering from insulin insufficiency; the elderly gentleman who has indecently touched a young woman during a ride on the Underground may still unconsciously want to prove to his mother that he is a man, or he may suffer from a gross distension of the prostate.

A good Prison Medical Officer must know the ailments of the body as well as of the mind, and has a unique opportunity to learn about the patient as a whole. Neither exclusively a physician nor yet a psychiatrist, he should be a truly complete medical practitioner. And more. For he will be increasingly concerned, not just to maintain and improve physical and mental health, but to help in that most challenging task of all —the rehabilitation of the offender and the prevention of further crime and unhappiness.

13

The Tutor Organizer

THIS chapter might almost equally have been headed 'The Psychologist'; almost but not quite, for though these two share certain common problems, I believe they may be more pronounced in the case of the Tutor Organizer, and more difficult to meet. On balance, therefore, the chapter goes to him.

I have already tried to show that all specialist staff in prison may sometimes feel isolated. The main job of keeping prisoners locked within walls, of stopping them from attacking others, and of making them conform to certain rules—all this is nothing to do with the specialist. He may sometimes be regarded as a bit of a frill—and he knows about these feelings. What is more, all worthwhile members of the rest of the staff are probably keen to do what rehabilitative work they can, and may resent Psychologists or Tutor Organizers 'straying' into this field. Psychologists? Why, they are the chaps who measure and test—well, let them get on with their measuring and testing. Tutor Organizers? They are the people who arrange for classes, arithmetic and French and current affairs—nothing wrong with that as long as they don't muck our prisoners about, and give them ideas.

There are psychologists and Tutor Organizers who are content to play these narrow roles, and there are others who are not. They argue that a psychologist is a person who is trained to understand the quirks of the mind, can help others to understand, and can make a very positive contribution in the actual treatment of delinquents. Tutor Organizers—or at least some—maintain that the job of an educationist is not just to take or arrange classes in arithmetic, French or current affairs, but to teach people how to live. And that includes teaching anti-social people how to live better lives.

Where such expansionist psychologists or Tutor Organizers are lucky enough to work under an understanding Governor (and/or doctor), all is well. But when they are not, then they may feel that the very real contribution which they believe they could make, is being wasted or ignored.

In such a case, the sum total of frustration in Tutor Organizer may be greater than that in the Psychologist. For one thing, the Psychologist is more closely integrated into the Prison Service than the Tutor Organizer. He can make something of a career in it by becoming a Senior Psychologist and later a Principal Psychologist; and attached to the Prison Commission there is a Chief Psychologist who is full-time, in a position to make policy, and to put the arguments in favour of an enlarged definition of the role of Psychologists if he thinks it right.

The Tutor Organizer has not one master, but two. He must please his local education authority—and it is they who pay the piper—and he must please the prison authorities who, ultimately, call the tune. Moreover, he has no career prospects whatever within the Prison Service. If he wants to get on, he must get out.

This is a great pity, I think. For even the man who has a real vocation for prison work may eventually be driven out of it by the economic needs of a growing family—even if he does not mind the feeling of being neither fish nor fowl, of not being wholly part of the place where he works, of being a life-long outsider. There is a case for integrating education into the Prison Service, for having Education Officers, Senior Education Officers, and so on—in fact, for making education in prisons a career. Integration should, however, be a two-way process. It is not only useful but essential that the rest of the staff, or at least some members of it, should be drawn into educational activities.

Quite a lot of them will have something to teach, something of themselves to give. And what is important in prison education is not only its formal content but the informal opportunities which it gives for working and discussing together, and for developing new relationships. An Officer may be regarded by prisoners as just another 'screw', but if he is an expert on hi-fi, or wood-carving, or pot-plants, and if he can share this interest, and infect a few prisoners with his enthusiasm, he will be regarded differently—and may in fact become different.

I am whole-heartedly on the side of those who see in prison education a chance to contribute towards rehabilitation. But I would never make education the whole or even the main rehabilitative instrument. Neither do I now share the view (which has sometimes been expressed to me) that there ought to be a more clearly defined policy for prison education.

Every prison has its own problems. The needs of Dartmoor prisoners, their collective temperament, their capacities, the possibilities which exist of drawing upon resources from outside —all these are quite different from the conditions which obtain at Wormwood Scrubs, or Wakefield, or Leyhill. Every Tutor Organizer has a different challenge to face and ought, within reason, to be allowed to meet it in his own way.

If, one day, we have smaller prisons, differently organized, knowing more about classification and grouping, then it may be that a more clear-cut policy would be required. Until then, I feel that what Tutor Organizers—particularly those who work in out-of-the-way prisons—need is encouragement, and again encouragement; the possibility of working closely with the rest of the staff, sitting in on staff conferences, being made to feel full members of the team; and plenty of opportunities of meeting their colleagues in order to compare notes and pick up fresh ideas. If they could have some training in psychology, and perhaps specially in social psychology and group dynamics, I believe this would be an additional and considerable advantage.

14
The Governor

THE Governor of a prison has powers which are acceptable in the father of small children but which would certainly be intolerable in the Prime Minister of a democratic country. However benevolent he may be, he is in fact a dictator, being at once chief administrator and judge, capable of punishing and rewarding those in his charge.

His powers are not, of course, unlimited, but the curbs which exist do not operate from below but from above. In a sense, it is the Prison Commissioners who are the agents of democracy, by laying down, and protecting, certain rights and privileges both of the prisoners and of the staff.

Nevertheless, the Governor's authority is considerable, and it is reinforced by the obedience which he is able, and indeed expected, to exact from all who are subordinate to him. And such are the restrictions on liberty and freedom of choice that there is no one below him who is not in a position of dependence.

Visitors to a particular prison often remark on how much morale varies with different Governors. The reason for this lies in the autocratic structure of the institution. Just as the microphone or the television camera will emphasize and exaggerate personal characteristics, so does the apparatus of power and discipline of which the Governor is head magnify his faults as well as his virtues. Thus even comparatively small differences in outlook and temperament between one man and another can lead to quite considerable changes in the atmosphere of the prison of which he is in charge.

Such power, even if checked and controlled from above, could lead to the emergence of highly unpleasant personality traits. The fact that it practically never does so is probably due partly to careful selection on the part of the Prison Commission, and partly to the strain of idealism (amounting sometimes to a tremendous sense of dedication) which many Governors exhibit, and which is fostered by the rehabilitative' aspects of their work—perhaps particularly by their experience of borstals and open prisons.

Indeed, their time at such institutions is often the happiest and most rewarding in their lives. It is heartbreaking how one can sometimes sense a man sadden as he rises from being in charge of a small borstal, moves up slightly chastened through one or two of the smaller prisons, and finally reaches his highest salary and most frustrating job as Governor of one of the huge and ancient monstrosities which serve as local prisons in our larger towns and cities.

Nobody likes these places, and dissatisfaction is made worse in recent times by the appalling pressure of numbers. Wearily the administrative routine clicks on, remands, receptions, transfers, discharges, and the Governor who (if he is good) probably wants to lift morale and engage in the struggle for the soul of the place, soon drowns in a sea of petitions, reports, instructions, minutes, requests for information, returns, amendments to standing orders, and so forth.

One day this really must change. One day, top salaries will have to be related to experience and flair, and not to the size of the institution. One day, there will have to be smaller prisons, more and better trained personnel, and greater freedom for the Governor to deal with people. And a chance for him to change his role.

For one of the most encouraging developments in the last few years has been the readiness, amongst the various grades of Governors, to re-examine old assumptions, to discard them when necessary, and to adjust their sights to new objectives. There is a kind of ferment going on, busily stirred by a few rebel spirits, a growing acceptance of the need to analyse relationships and to understand behaviour not just as immediately expressed but against the background of the forces which may influence it.

All this is leading to a demand for more specialized training, a desire to understand group tensions, their modification and constructive use, and perhaps most difficult of all, a willingness to replace reliance on obedience by the art of fostering spontaneous co-operation.

But the chances of trying out in practice newly discovered or re-discovered skills remain comparatively slender. It is very difficult to do at all in large local prisons. And those who have tried it in training prisons and borstals know that it may trigger off a whole chain of new problems: the need to reconsider authority and responsibility, classification and deliberate grouping, and the administration and structure of prison itself.

Ideas about prisons and the régime within them have been changing throughout this century. But the period of transformation which is now being entered into, and which—for the first time—will be accompanied by the scientific assessments of results, promises to be more painful but ultimately also more rewarding than any other.

Governors are leaders. They are, or should be, in the forefront of change. But they are also members of a service, part of a system, and sometimes victims of the pressure which is generated within it. They are expected to set an example, to think about the needs of the staff, to take into account the wants of the prisoners. They are supposed to be wise, humane, fair, good at human relations, and always prepared to give help, guidance and support to others.

But they, too, need help and support. And they are entitled to get this, not only from their superiors but also from penal reformers and from the public at large. They, and indeed all who work in prisons, deserve not only recognition of all the difficulties and complexities of their work, but a constant assurance and reassurance of the infinite worth of its ultimate purpose—the reconstruction of the human personality.

Part IV
PRISON PROBLEMS

15
Power and Discipline

THE qualities of a totalitarian political régime have been described often enough: the concentration of power in the hands of a ruling clique; the removal of any effective opposition; the imposition by those in power of their will, if needs be by force; and the proliferation of bureaucratic controls made necessary through the attempt at detailed control of economic, political, public and even private life. In place of democratic rights and privileges such as freedom of association and assembly, or collective bargaining and the right to strike, there is complete direction of labour; a strict censorship; the encouragement of informers; and finally the attempt to impose an ideology.

The front along which such a régime breaks down most easily is the ideological one, particularly if the majority of people have no real desire to share the values and aspirations of the ruling clique. Most of them may outwardly conform and even become apparently good party members but the distinction between private sentiments and public affirmations is so large that if there is an opportunity to gratify the former, it will be taken. So far from feeling guilty at breaking rules, there may be a sense of achievement for having cocked a snook at those in power. The police, knowing this state of affairs, not unnaturally distrust all civilians, the civilians distrust and resent the police, and there tends to grow up that general air of suspicion which so often poisons the atmosphere in a dictatorship.

93

The analogy with prison could be taken further. It is not an exact analogy, of course, for the power which is exercised in a prison stems from the Prison Commissioners, and they are servants of the public, directly responsible to Parliament through the Home Secretary. And when they exercise their delegated powers, they do so as men and women of high purpose and ideals, conscientious, self-critical, enlightened, and anxious to do their job in the best and most responsible manner.

None of this prevents large maximum security prisons from being rather like miniature totalitarian states. Why should this be so?

The answer, I believe, lies partly in the attitude of the public towards the offender, and partly in the nature of power itself and the circumstances in which it is exercised.

A large majority of the public wishes to see the convicted offender punished. The perpetual shortage of work, of money for suitable buildings, of facilities of all kinds—these all derive ultimately from a perhaps unacknowledged desire for revenge and retribution. So does the idea of imprisonment itself.

But prison is not just a wall around so many human beings held captive—it is a system of power, designed to compel them to do this and to refrain from doing that. It is a discipline, imposed and ultimately backed by the threat of force.

There is nothing wrong in discipline itself. Indeed, it is essential and must be practiced by everyone to some degree —from the housewife who takes her place in the queue to the soldier who goes on a dangerous mission. But it can usually only be taught if the learner can identify with the teacher and if his basic aim is understood and accepted. It is the child who loves, and is loved by, his parents, who learns obedience; it is the soldier who wants to defend his country, who trusts his superiors and who may even hope one day to emulate them, who will willingly comply with orders; and it is the citizen who has confidence in his Government who will accept stern measures and sacrifice.

But the prisoner in a maximum security prison, especially the recidivist prisoner, tends to see the prison staff as inflictors of punishment, as coercers, as instruments of a hostile society. If he can, he will cling to some injustice, fancied or real, and so help his resistance. For just as an occupied nation will produce a resistance movement, so do prisoners form underground movements, and even such individual exploits as escapes can often be seen as a demonstration of defiance, a dramatic act of rebellion rather than a realistic attempt to get away.

This attitude is not adopted without reason. For society *does* want to punish the prisoner, the Prison Commissioners *are* the servants of the public, and even though every attempt is made by them to introduce the rehabilitative element, it has little chance to survive under the kind of pressure which builds up in a large maximum security prison. The battery of orders and prohibitions, the rewards and punishments which seek to regulate compliance, the massive and palpable power and weight of authority, the passivity into which prisoners are forced, the impersonality of the big institutions—all these are almost insurmountable obstacles between the aim of rehabilitation and its achievement.

To this must be added the fact that such an authoritarian régime reduces those upon whom it presses to a state of irresponsibility. And since most prisoners, certainly most recidivist prisoners, are already irresponsible, putting them into a large maximum security prison is rather like locking a group of drunkards into a brewery. If some of them nevertheless succeed in staying sober, it will not necessarily be because the brewery was the right place into which to put them.

The nineteenth century thinkers and administrators to whom we owe our prison buildings, and therefore to some extent our system, had aims quite different from those the Prison Commissioners have now. The buildings, the system, the ways by which compliance was enforced—they suited nineteenth century aims. It is difficult to graft new aims on to these old foundations. For people cannot be ordered into maturity; they cannot be disciplined into it, they cannot even be flogged into it.

A different system is needed. Small prisons, and small groups within small prisons. Small enough groups to be able to relax discipline and to introduce some democracy. Small enough to have some rules jointly made and jointly accepted, to encourage responsibility, and to provide a climate in which prison officers can lead and need not suppress.

95

16
Punishments and Rewards

WHAT are stimuli to action, and what deterrents? The answers to these questions, and the assumptions behind them, may influence the nature and quality of a whole civilization.

In an acquisitive society like ours, metaphors such as the carrot and the stick come readily to the lips of many, and the elevating image of man as a donkey may be implied in the way in which most of our industrial and social institutions are assumed to be working. The theme of self-interest, or perhaps of enlightened self-interest, is one which politicians do not easily forget even if they sometimes remember that the promise of blood, sweat and tears proved to be remarkably effective as a call to action.

To those who tend to see life in certain simple terms, the carrot is an appeal to greed, the stick to fear, and both unquestionably work. But even accepting their premise for the moment, is the desire to be better dressed, to have a larger car and a bigger house, really just simple greed? How much are possessions valued for themselves, and how much as symbols of status in relation to other people?

Here we get into deeper water. It is fairly clear that the donkey seems to like at least some carrots not because he wants to eat them but because he is a snob. To some extent, we are all keeping up with the Joneses. Nor is this just a suburban or middle-class pre-occupation. It can be observed in such matters as negotiations between employers and workers. Quite a few arguments in collective bargaining may be based on comparisons with other workers and other wage-awards. Provincial bus-drivers and provincial printers may feel strongly that they are 'worth' just as much as their London colleagues. And in this desire to maintain status, there can be sensed the need to feel esteemed and approved of which may be as important as the money itself.

But the real trouble is that the original premise simply does not hold good. Donkeys are notoriously obstinate, and so are human beings. Money, honours, rewards, threats, punishments, carrots and sticks of every kind may leave the saint and the rebel absolutely cold. Nonconformists may continue not to conform in spite of the pressures which society may bring to bear on them—because they do not accept the standards and values of that society. Rewards and punishment given by an authority which is not freely accepted may not only fail but have the opposite of the intended effect. Conscientious objectors or demonstrators at atomic missile stations may even be proud of the punishment they receive since they reject the authority which imposes it.

At last we arrive at the problem in prison. If the staff of a prison can win acceptance from prisoners, even in the face of initial opposition, the incentives and disincentives can support the rehabilitative aim. If they cannot, then rewards and punishments may satisfy the sense of justice of the staff, but may be illusory as far as support for the aims of the régime is concerned. Indeed, they may work against them, in the sense that favour by the authorities may be viewed with suspicion by prisoners, and punishment may confer distinction.

But what matters is not only by whom, and in what circumstances, a system of rewards and punishments is operated; it is also important what the rewards and punishments themselves actually are, and how their nature affects those who give and receive them.

It is a lamentable fact that two of the punishments still carried out in prison directly contradict the constructive aims embodied in the prison rules. How can the objectives of reform and rehabilitation be carried out in the same place in which one prisoner may be flogged with a heavy lash, and another killed by the hangman's rope?

The carrying out, or even the connivance in the carrying out by others, of such punishments implicates the whole of the prison staff and vitally detracts from the kind of positive authority which they may be able to exercise. The fact that the prison service is expected at once to do social work and also to inflict punishment is unfair, an anachronism, a reflection of the conflict of ideas which still exists about imprisonment itself.

This is not to say that firmness has no place in dealing with prisoners. But there are degrees of firmness beyond which it is not possible to go without at one point turning yourself into their enemy. And you cannot be friend and enemy at the same time.

It is bad enough that flogging a prisoner still exists as a punishment. It is worse that it is carried out in the very place in which attempts at rehabilitation are made. It is worse still that it must be inflicted by a prison officer; and it becomes almost incomprehensible when one remembers that in practice prisoners are only flogged for attacking a prison officer: for at the receiving end, it must sometimes look very like assault and counter-assault—not punishment by an impartial outsider but straightforward retaliation by one of the men attacked, part of the war between the two sides.

The Governor must preside at the ritual as the prisoner is strapped into position and rendered helpless, ready for the flogging. The Medical Officer must be present, too, prepared to intervene should the shock prove too great for the prisoner's heart.

Though I know Governors and doctors who do not seem to mind this spectacle, I know many others for whom it is an ordeal which they dread and loathe, and who are convinced that it is as wrong as it is ill-designed to make an explosively aggressive individual less hostile.

It is perhaps no accident that quite a lot of the prisoners who have been flogged strongly believe in it. Of several men who affirmed this to me, I particularly remember one who was most vehement in his protestations. 'It did me good,' he exclaimed, and when I asked him whether he had subsequently contained his violent behaviour, he scornfully denied it. And to his way of thinking, it may have done him good—by confirming his opinion of authority, and of himself.

98

In the case of an execution, at least the sentence itself is not carried out by prison officers. But prison officers must still guard the prisoner till the very minute of his death, must prevent his escape, must acquiesce in the act of taking his life—as must so many others, the governor, the doctor, the chaplain.

It is only fair to point out that the Homicide Act of 1957 has greatly reduced the number of executions (without, incidentally, the murder rate going up) and that corporal punishment is now very rarely carried out.

I am an opponent of hanging and flogging, and not only for the reasons implicit in what I have said so far. But even if I were not, I would consider even the remote possibility of such punishments being inflicted inside prison as a major obstacle in the way of a rehabilitative régime.

Nevertheless, I would not abolish corporal punishment overnight. For it is quite clear that many prison officers are genuinely convinced that the threat of corporal punishment is a protection for them. If it really were so, then the case for abolishing it would be harder to defend. There is, however, no evidence to suggest that officers really are better protected, and there *is* evidence that men who have been flogged have attacked again. All the same, the feeling of being protected is there, and should not be removed without the introduction of other measures—otherwise the sense of grievance and the strain which officers experience might be exacerbated, and there might be recourse to unofficial beatings.

What has to be done, I believe, is to bring about a general reduction in tension. We are back at the central problem of small prisons, and small, easily manageable and properly selected groups. In addition, there may have to be sufficient Governor/staff discussions for anxiety and resentment to be relieved by free expression, and for the feeling to develop that the load is being shouldered jointly.

The rest of the punishments include loss of remission, loss of earnings, and two penalties reminiscent of childhood: restricted diet and solitary confinement. Rewards consist mainly of privileges such as greater freedom of association; not, in themselves, exactly powerful incentives.

Whether these rewards and punishments really succeed in modifying and changing behaviour may in the end depend more on the liking and respect which prisoners develop for the Governor and his staff than on the extent to which officially defined sticks and carrots are used, or not used.

17
Work and Leisure

THERE is no single reason why there is so little work in ordinary maximum security prisons. It is a problem which bedevils not only this country—officials of other prison systems have similar difficulties.

For one thing, it is intrinsically difficult to find a continuous flow of work for an immobile labour force of (in England and Wales) some 26,000 workers whose intelligence and capacity is well below average. Prisons are horribly permanent but not necessarily well placed to take advantage of new developments in light industry. They are so overcrowded that it may sometimes be impossible to build enough suitable workshops. And because of the expense to the public, the authorities dare not put in good, up-to-date and possibly costly equipment unless they are quite sure of getting the sort of long-term contract which would justify the outlay. Needless to say, such contracts do not fall off trees.

That is why the Prison Commissioners (while making every effort to obtain work from private industry) have to rely largely on Government contracts of a kind which are clearly repeatable. There is always stiff competition, not only from commercial undertakings but also from organizations which provide work for the handicapped, such as Remploy or Institutes for the Blind, which, like the Prison Commissioners, have to rely on a comparatively narrow range of manufactures capable of being produced by those whom they employ.

Over and above that, the employment of prisoners may from time to time meet opposition, both from employers and from trade unions (from the latter particularly concerning work outside prison walls), and this may understandably be considerable where there are local pockets of unemployment. Shortage of staff, acute until recently, is a further limiting factor since it means a single-shift system with consequent restrictions on the number of hours that prisoners can spend outside their cells.

Finally, there is the practice of concentrating the most interesting and constructive type of work in training prisons. This is a consequence of the policy of creaming off the better personalities—a policy which is possibly open to question on grounds which will be discussed later. The result is that local prisons not only have less work, and less constructive work, but also fewer of the better and more capable types of prisoners—all of which impairs morale and atmosphere in their workshops.

Learning to work, or perhaps more precisely, learning how to work may be an important part of the process of socialization and rehabilitation. But it is important to understand the reasons behind a prisoner's poor work-record, as well as the nature and function of work itself. At least so far as adult recidivists are concerned, I do not believe that forcing them to work will, by itself, bring about any positive changes either in work habits or in personality.

Work habits are often acquired early in life, and bad work habits may have their roots deep in childhood. The life-histories of many delinquent children show truancy, and of adult recidivists, frequent changes of jobs, an inability to stick to anything, which may shade off into complete work shyness (by no means necessarily the equivalent of laziness).

Persistent truanting from school and constant changes of jobs are not the same thing but there are similarities. The reason may lie in an unsatisfactory relationship between parents and child, setting the pattern for an unsatisfactory relationship between child and teacher, and foreshadowing a similar relationship with employers and others in authority. Or there may be strife between the parents, and such resultant conflict within the child that performance at school (or, subsequently, at work) is poor, and there is withdrawal from the challenge of competition. Again, the child or young adult may be so pre-occupied with himself and his own problems that he remains isolated and unpopular, or is driven to seek popularity among the less well-adjusted members of his age-group by becoming a leader in acts of defiance and hostility against teachers, employers, grown-ups, and finally society itself.

The combinations and permutations of circumstances may be considerable, and of such intensity that the reaction is equally strong. Such reactions, repeated often enough, eventually become established behaviour and part of the make-up of the personality. Ideally, in every recidivist prisoner the reasons why illegitimate behaviour is preferred to legitimate conduct, crime to work, anti-social activities to friendly co-operation with others ought to be examined before ever treatment, and the place which work itself should have in it, is planned.

To all of us, work is a highly significant activity. It is a service which we can offer, and which brings us many different returns. It enables us to earn a living and perhaps keep a family. It gives us a recognizable function whereby we can be useful to others, and others can be useful to us. It gives us status—and when this can be increased, the increase will be reflected in the degree of work satisfaction which is felt. It gives us a social role, that is, a certain relationship to others—and the nature of that relationship, too, influences work satisfaction. It gives us a sense of power, of mastery at least over some events, and perhaps over some people. The more successful we are at work, the greater the returns in some of these interlinking aspects of our relationship with others, and the more agreeable our own image in the mirror of their attitude to us.

Conversely, if we are out of work, and particularly if we are unemployed for outward economic reasons, we feel—and are—rejected, unwanted, useless. We have no function, no role, no status, we can make no contribution. And we are in danger of losing our self-respect.

And now back to the recidivist. The recidivist has no real self-respect and he is not really respected by others—at least, not by society in general, nor by authority. In ninety-nine cases out of a hundred, crime does not pay—work pays much better. Persistent work may bring success, perhaps admiration—persistent crime, failure, condemnation, punishment. Work implies, in many different ways, a constructive, a fruitful, a social relationship with others—crime implies, in equally many ways, a destructive, an anti-social relationship.

The importance of work in prison cannot, therefore, be over-emphasized. But it is not just a question of providing something to do, of filling the long hours—though being occupied is always better than being unoccupied. It is necessary to provide an acceptable function, status, and social role so that as these aspects of the relationship with others change and develop, the prisoner's inner picture of himself—his self-respect—also changes and improves.

Three things, I believe, are necessary for this: work which can be recognized as purposeful and useful; an instructor, or foreman, of good personality—a figure of authority, whom it is easy to accept; and a small working-group, carefully selected, and within which work is so arranged that there can develop some degree of mutual inter-dependency.

Even if these conditions could be fulfilled, work should not be relied upon to be the main rehabilitative instrument. If much damage was done in childhood, it may be necessary to get down to this by group therapy and perhaps by individual sessions. By every possible means, there has to be generated a climate of faith in change, pressures which make for change, and of these, work is but one; though ultimately attitudes to work (since they reflect attitudes to self) may be the decisive test.

Leisure, too, has its part to play, and the considerations which apply to it are similar. A film show, a concert given by others, entertainments in which there are no participants but only passive spectators—these are not important. But concerts which the prisoners give, plays which they perform themselves are of value, particularly when they lead to good co-operation with other prisoners and with members of the staff. It may be far better to have five small and primitive stages where small groups can play to other small groups than one big and elaborate stage (or screen) where professionals perform to a large audience. And if female parts are required, there is no strong reason why the Chief Officer's daughter or the doctor's wife, if they are so minded, should not oblige;[1] no strong arguments against and quite a few in favour.

[1] In fact, they already do so in some institutions.

18
Love and Isolation

SOME aspects of the stunting of the personality which may occur when prisoners are locked up for lengthy periods have already been discussed. We know that there are long-term prisoners who may come to fear freedom, and to lose—at least temporarily—what little initiative and self-reliance they may have had. That is why the Prison Commissioners' experiment extending the hostel system towards the end of a long sentence is particularly to be welcomed. Under this system, selected prisoners can do a few months' normal work in outside factories or offices, returning every night to a hostel within, or close to, the prison—a period of semi-liberty between a long spell of captivity and complete freedom.

Prolonged imprisonment, however, has other serious results; notably a drastic diminution of the possibility of expressing and experiencing love and affection, and the impossibility of having heterosexual intercourse. Tenderness and desire are, or should be, part of the same range of feelings, and to be deprived for long periods of opportunities for expressing them, or of evoking them in someone else, may be damaging—especially in certain individuals.

Such attention as this problem has received has tended to concentrate on the question of sexual tension and its relief. Undoubtedly, persons with a strong sexual drive must find a long sentence of imprisonment particularly difficult. They are probably more often men than women; not only because there are so many more male long-term prisoners but also because for women a direct sexual outlet is not always quite so important.

The possibility of sublimating these drives in prison through some sort of creative work or leisure is not great. It is certainly not impossible in a busy training prison, with plenty of art classes, amateur dramatics and similar activities. But in an ordinary local prison, the chances of successful sublimation of this kind must be small.

In a woman's prison, there may consequently be a good many emotional friendships some of which probably have a sexual basis but which do not necessarily result in physical contact. In a men's prison, there may be more overt homosexuality, and more attempts at expressing it physically. There is also likely to be more sex talk. Indeed, sex is probably the most popular topic of conversation, outstripping even food.

But for most prisoners who suffer from sexual tension, the only possibility of outlet is masturbation. This may afford some relief but it can also have its dangers. Quite a few offenders cannot face reality anyway. They do not see themselves, and their relationship to others, as they really are, and they may have great difficulties in putting themselves into someone else's shoes. They tend to be exclusively concerned with their own reactions to life, preoccupied with the satisfaction of their own needs, and without much thought for the feeling of others.

If this type of person is sent to prison, his estrangement from reality, from the world of others, may become even greater. For prison may be a shelter, not only in the sense of providing food and a roof over his head, but also in cushioning him from life and its network of personal relationships.

This narrowing and impoverishment of existence over a prolonged period may lead to a further deterioration of personality and the downward process is unlikely to be impeded by habitual masturbation, when fantasy takes the place of a real person, and self-gratification becomes the only aim.

The capacity to form good personal relationships and to give and receive enduring affection is first learned in childhood. It depends upon the type of relationship which develops between parents and child, and since many recidivists seem to have had unsatisfactory childhood experiences, it is not surprising that they so often fail to build stable bonds later on.

A high proportion of recidivists are actually homeless, and they seem to be homeless because they are lonely and isolated persons, and not the other way round. A prolonged period of imprisonment may drive such people further in upon themselves. I imagine this must be particularly so in certain continental prisons where solitary confinement is still quite common. But even for those who have managed to build some enduring relationship, a long spell in prison may be damaging. There are quite a few married men serving Preventive Detention, but there are not so very many whose marriage manages to survive the long years of separation intact.

Various attempts have therefore been made to avoid a complete severance of personal and sometimes of sexual relationships. Most modern prison systems provide facilities for visits by wives, husbands, fiancées or friends, usually one, and more rarely two visits, per month. This is also the practice in English local prisons. But in the course of an inquiry into marital relationships of prisoners in the United States[1] it was revealed that although twenty-three state prisons allow only one visit a month, forty-one prisons provide for four or more visits per month, sometimes lasting for half or even a full day. Admittedly, the longer visits appear to be exceptional.

In some South American countries, wives or permanent mistresses are allowed to visit their husbands in prison specifically for the purpose of sexual intercourse. A preferable way may be the Swedish system of granting regular home leave to prisoners.

A leave system exists also in this country where it is used for prisoners serving two years or upwards—but only one home-leave is normally allowed, and that towards the end of the sentence. It is for the specific purpose of preparing for final release.

I believe that the use and purpose of home-leave should be widened as part of a general attempt to broaden the basis of rehabilitation. Similar considerations should apply to letters to and from prisoners. At the moment, the extension of visiting

[1] *Marital Relationships of Prisoners.* By Eugene Zemans and Ruth Shonle Cavan, Journal of Criminal Law, Criminology and Police Section. Vol 49, No. 1, May-June 1958.

and letter-writing facilities is made very difficult because of the appalling overcrowding. Letters have to be censored and visits to be supervised. But by no means every prisoner constitutes a security problem—in fact, the majority do not. Those who do may have to have special regulations, but for the others, increasing contacts with relations ought to be possible. And to return once again to one of the main themes which run through this book: the problem of security would be much easier to solve in small prisons than in large ones.

Letters to and from wives, husbands, children, parents and intimate friends are an important link with the outside world. It may well be that deep-rooted delinquency, sexual and social maladjustment are often part and parcel of the same syndrome, affecting relationships with others at many points. Where such relationships are still good and sound, then surely it would be wise to make great efforts to preserve them, and, if possible, to utilize them in the process of re-socialization.

Part V
PATTERN OF THE FUTURE

Introductory Note

IN this last part of the book, I shall try to examine how the régime in a maximum security prison could be changed so that the pressures which are generated could be used constructively, and harnessed to the regenerative processes which I believe ought to be set in motion. But the régime in any one prison reflects to a considerable degree the notions which underlie the prison system as a whole. The two are so closely connected that it is not possible to change one without also affecting the other.

The changes, however, need not be abrupt. They could be introduced gradually, tested for their effectiveness, and if found satisfactory, taken further. The end result would not be a prison Utopia. There would certainly be many failures. But I believe there could also be many more successes, particularly amongst recidivists. And it is the recidivist who is the real test, for eighty per cent of first offenders do not offend again, no matter what sentence is imposed upon them. They cannot be chalked up as specific prison successes any more than they can be regarded as proving the virtue of probation, or any other method open to the courts.

No, it is by what happens to recidivists that prisons must be measured; and it is for them that treatment may have to be deepened.

19
The System Now

PRISONS and borstals in England and Wales are administered by one central organization—the Prison Commission. Prisons themselves are divided into Central Prisons, Regional Prisons, Corrective Training Prisons and Local Prisons. (Borstals and Detention Centres for young offenders also come under the Prison Commission.) One of the Central Prisons (Leyhill) and several of the Regional and Local Prisons are open.

Central Prisons are for prisoners serving long sentences—in theory for those with sentences of three years and upwards but in practice, owing to overcrowding, long sentence recidivists serving as much as four years may have to be kept in Local Prisons. Central Prisons include amongst ot hers Dartmoor, Parkhurst, and parts of Wormwood Scrubs.

Regional Prisons are training institutions for selected prisoners serving twelve months or more. First offenders with the appropriate length of sentence have a good chance of being sent to a Regional Prison but recidivists are not excluded. Selection is made on the basis of personality. Regional Prisons have plenty of work, and all kinds of training facilities. They are very hopeful places, the best known of them being Wakefield and Maidstone, each with a separate open camp.

Corrective Training Prisons are prisons, or parts of prisons, set aside for those who receive a sentence of Corrective Training —i.e. younger recidivists over twenty-one who are still considered trainable. Their sentence may last from two to four years. Regional Prisons often serve as Corrective Training Prisons also.

Local Prisons make up the great majority of our prisons. Most of them are maximum security prisons, and some of them are very large. Five at present house more than a thousand prisoners (Liverpool, Manchester, Pentonville, Wandsworth and Wormwood Scrubs), and at least five more house over five hundred. Every prisoner is sent to a local prison on first committal, and the majority have to stay there since they are not eligible for transfer to one of the other prisons or an open institution.

An official pamphlet[1] comments on conditions in Local Prisons as follows:

'So far as concerns convicted prisoners, therefore, their population consists solely of those who by reason of their character or length of sentence are ineligible for full training.'

And elsewhere

'[Local] Prisons were built, for the most part a hundred years or more ago, to serve the purpose of the deterrent and repressive régime of their time, and they are little suited to the purposes of today.'

Later on, the pamphlet states

'... those remaining in local prisons present an unhopeful prospect for training. That the normal conditions are not helpful has been made clear, and at present they are made worse by two factors. Overcrowding means a general slowing down of tempo and clogging of routine, while the concomitant of "three in a cell", which has been deliberately restricted to these prisons, can be defended on no other ground than sheer necessity. It has also proved impossible to recruit the large number of additional prison officers who would be required to man local prisons on a shift basis covering the whole active day, as is done in other types of prison: the prisoners' working hours are therefore, on

[1] Prisons and Borstals. H.M.S.O. 1957.

average, only about 22–25 hours a week, though some workshops may work 30 hours or more.'

Since this was written, overcrowding has become much worse. The daily average population in prisons and borstals is now over 26,000 (compared with about 10,000 before the war); and some 6,000 men have to sleep three in a cell. With so many hands to occupy, it has not been possible to prolong the average working week, and occasionally it may be so little as twenty hours.

Recruitment of staff, on the other hand, has improved and may improve further as a result of the recommendations on pay made by the Wynn-Parry Committee (*see* Chapter 7).

To sum up: most of the more hopeful cases amongst the prisoners have a good chance of getting to Regional Prisons or to Open Prisons, always provided their sentences are not too short or too long. Those with really long sentences will sooner or later get into Central Prisons where certain facilities exist to make these long sentences more tolerable. Local prisons are left with a mass of short-term prisoners[1] (fifty per cent of all prison sentences are for three months or less, and twenty-five per cent are between two and five weeks). But they must also cope with those who get longer sentences and who are not considered suitable for special training; and with a number of recidivists with very long sentences who must serve at least a part of their sentence there.

The general picture that emerges is of a system designed to separate the better personalities amongst the prisoners, who are fortunate enough to have a manageable sentence, from the worst personalities, many of whom will have very short (and some very long) sentences. For it must not be thought that those who get very short terms of imprisonment are mostly people who are basically sound. The contrary is often true. A great many of the short-termers are recidivists for whom all sorts of other methods, such as probation or fines, may already have been tried without success. They are often inadequates, sometimes with psychopathic personality traits—petty offenders, down-and-outs, alcoholics—and their rehabilitation may

---

[1] See also p. 21.

present considerable difficulties, and may sometimes be impossible in the present state of our knowledge.

Another point which is relevant here is, of course, the actual size of the prison. In a small prison, it is possible to do things which are very difficult to achieve in a large prison; and, as we have seen, many of our local prisons are not only old and unsuitable buildings but they are also very large.

Inevitably, but perhaps unfortunately, promotion in the Prison Service has become related to the size of these institutions. To reach the rank of Governor, Class I, a man must usually be prepared to be in charge of a large prison—even if he feels uneasily that he might not be able to do much good there. Thus the structure of the Prison Service has itself come to reflect, in a way, the type of buildings considered appropriate in the mid-nineteenth century. And, for Governors, administrative skills are more important, and more remunerative, than social skills. This may have been all right in former days but now, when it is clear that training and some understanding of individual and social psychology is becoming more necessary, the position is more doubtful.

What I should like to see is the gradual development of the existing prison system so that, instead of having seventy institutions, some of them large, some medium, and some small, we shall eventually have something like double the number of institutions, all of them small. Of these, some might be exclusively for prisoners serving very short sentences, some for those with very long sentences, and one or two for very difficult psychopaths.

All the rest would be for prisoners who do not fall into any of these categories. There would be no attempt to separate the good personalities from the less good. On the contrary, the whole object of classification would become an attempt to see that each institution has a heterogeneous group of prisoners. Within each prison, I envisage sub-groups, also heterogeneous, so that in all group activities, the better personalities can support the worse, and no group consists entirely of good or entirely of bad characters.

This system would demand a reorganization of the Prison Service. Beginning at the top, I should like to see promotion to

Governor on the basis of personality, with really adequate training and a considerable degree of social skill ranking high. There may have to be a simplification in grading from three to two, with the highest grade (Governor Class I) going to those who are in charge of training institutions. The word 'training' in this context might apply to staff rather than prisoner, and one could envisage a number of particularly skilful Governors being in charge of a higher complement of staff, supernumery to the regular establishment. A proportion of these might be doing post-initial training (i.e. not the initial training course[1] itself but a subsequent period of training where they learn as they work); others might be doing refresher courses.

There would no doubt have to be consequential reorganizations in the lower ranks of the service. But though sub-gradings may have to be simplified, more separate units should give more staff members opportunities for initiative and promotion might well become quicker.

None of these changes would be easy to make. Nor would I advocate them unless fairly convincing proof were forthcoming that the new ways might give better results.

Fortunately, criminology has advanced sufficiently to enable us to do just this. We can proceed on the basis of a controlled experiment. If such an experiment showed that better results would be forthcoming, then the old system could gradually be adapted, and a new system developed.

The foundations for such a developing system are already contained in the White Paper on Penal Practice[2] which contains a series of highly important proposals.

---

[1] Initial training and some refresher courses are already being given at the Staff College and the Officers Training School, both at Wakefield.
[2] Penal Practice in a Changing Society. H.M.S.O. 1959.

20
The System Developing

THE White Paper has come about owing to the fact that an exceptional chairman of the Prison Commission[1] happened to serve under an exceptional Home Secretary.[2] The result is a document which is likely to go down as a landmark in penal history. In its way, it may have as profound an effect on future developments as the Gladstone Committee had towards the end of the last century.

I intend here to discuss only two of the many concepts and ideas which are outlined in it. They are particularly germane to the proposals I want to make. But this does not mean there are not many others which are of very great importance.

First of all, it is intended to set up a number of Remand and Observation Centres. The first of these is likely to be completed within a few years.

At the moment, prisoners remanded in custody are kept in local prisons, and if the courts require information on the personality and background of such prisoners, it must be supplied by personnel from local prisons.

To illustrate how much administrative and sometimes diagnostic work is involved, an extract from the latest Report of the Prison Commissioners[3] is given below:

Receptions (Men)   1957

I Receptions of untried prisoners on commitment for trial or in course of hearing before a Magistrates' Court   24,272

---

[1] Sir Lionel Fox, C.B., M.C.   [2] Rt. Hon. R. A. Butler, C.H., M.P.
[3] Report of the Commissioners of Prisons for the Year 1957. H.M.S.O. 1958.

II Reception on commitment following conviction,
     for inquiry or to await sentence   8,202

There is one other figure that is of interest in this connexion
The same Report states that in 1957, 10,438 persons (about
forty per cent of prisoners on remand or for trial) were remanded
in prison but *not* subsequently sentenced to imprisonment.

The White Paper envisages that all these cases would
eventually be sent to Remand Centres, to which would be
attached Observation and Classification Centres, designed for
the purpose and staffed by expert diagnostic teams.

This would not only ease the pressure on local prisons
quite considerably but also provide far better information for
the courts than has hitherto been available. The result should
eventually be reflected in the sentencing policy of the courts,
and may possibly go some way towards reducing the number
of very short and perhaps also of very long sentences. (Regarding
the latter, the White Paper also envisages a review of Preventive
Detention—very long sentences of between five and fourteen
years, given to older recidivists, not because of the gravity of
their offence but because of the number of their previous
convictions.)

But Observation and Classification Centres could also do
the work of allocating convicted prisoners to different prisons
—a job which is necessarily also done in local prisons at the
moment.

At this point, the White Paper puts its proposals in the
following way:

'The Commissioners wish to develop a system of classification which is based more on the study of the personalities
of offenders and less on objective criteria such as previous
convictions and sentences.'

And later

'A more refined system of classification and allocation
would be of no value without suitable establishments in
which prisoners, *particularly recidivists* [my italics] with
medium-length sentences, can be given the type of training
which they require and which cannot be adequately provided

117

in the local prisons. To meet this need it will be necessary to build a number of additional training prisons.'

I differ from these proposals only in that I would not envisage Training Prisons for recidivists. As I have tried to explain, I believe a rehabilitative atmosphere might be very difficult to achieve in an institution solely for recidivists. In my view, we need the better personalities to build upon, to use in all forms of group activities and also to influence prisoner public opinion.

Secondly, the White Paper foresees a complete modernization and reorganization of local prisons, and the provision of up-to-date training facilities of all kinds. Finally, in the largest prisons,

'some of which now hold over 1,000 prisoners, it may well be that reconstruction should include some form of sub-division into units of a more manageable size.'

The value of smaller units is therefore already officially recognized and part of Government policy. My own proposals would merely take this policy further and—provided experiments show that the results would justify such a course—would eventually draw the logical conclusions in terms of the prison system and the Prison Service.

To clarify further the point about the distribution of personalities within the prison system, it is helpful to divide prisoners into categories according to characteristics. For example,

A—those with reasonably good personalities
B—those with less good personalities
C—those with difficult personalities (including some who show psychopathic traits)
D—those with very difficult personalities (grossly unstable psychopaths)

According to the present system, a Regional or other Training Prison or an Open Prison is likely to contain many As, some Bs, and very few Cs. By contrast, a local prison is likely to contain comparatively few As, a fair number of Bs, many Cs, and a small percentage of Ds. The As (many of whom are probably first offenders) are likely to do well anywhere, or so I would guess. The relatively small number of Bs and Cs in Training or Open Prisons may do slightly better there; but there are very many more of them in a local prison, and I would surmise they would fare rather badly. The Ds are probably beyond help and constitute (and produce) treatment difficulties out of all proportion to their small number.

Phase I of my proposal would be to build, as part of the extensive building programme already envisaged in the White Paper, one small prison for not more than 150 prisoners, with a special treatment programme. The prisoners would constitute a balanced mixture of As, Bs and Cs. The hypothesis is that the As would do well, but that a comparatively large percentage of Bs and Cs would also do relatively well; and that the total result would be better than that of a similar number of the same prisoners from a Local and a Training or Open Prison combined.

If this theory proves correct—i.e. that firstly by improved treatment methods, and secondly by underpinning mixed B and C groups with As—a real improvement can be made in the total number of prisoners who are rehabilitated, then I believe the Prison Commission would be justified in pushing this system slowly ahead, making sure all the time that results justify what they are doing. Phase II could then be entered —i.e. the extension of this system.

I put this proposal forward with the utmost seriousness, knowing that the Prison Commissioners are perfectly prepared nowadays to carry out just such experiments. Since there are really two main propositions in the one hypothesis—new treatment methods and a different grouping of prisoners—they may prefer to test each main proposition separately so that we know the relative importance of each. But it is the two combined that I believe would give the best difference; and this, too, can be tested.

If the hypothesis is proved, a new prison system could gradually be developed. Training prisons, and Open Prisons as we now know them might slowly disappear—and this might well arouse some opposition, for these institutions are the pride and joy of the Prison Commissioners as well as of Penal

Reformers. Open Prisons in particular are hailed universally and rightly as the great and humane twentieth-century contribution to rehabilitation.

Of course they will go on in some form. The most that I would conjecture is that we may find we are not using them in the best way at the moment. By putting the best personalities amongst prisoners into special institutions, we may be winning victories which are too easy while leaving ourselves with an almost impossible task with all the rest.

Conceivably, Open Prisons might be used one day for longer-term prisoners of the A, B and C types who have already benefited by some training in closed institutions—indeed, it may be that most such prisoners ought ideally to go through at least a few weeks of an Open Prison before final release.

A word about expense. One small prison for 150 inmates such as I have suggested would be relatively costly to build. The larger prison for 300 at present envisaged in the White Paper is a better proposition economically when one takes into account the cost of land, of construction, and of administration.

Nevertheless, I would plead for at least one specially built small maximum security institution. If we are going to carry out an experiment which might lead to major changes in the prison system, and to a reduction of recidivism, let us give it the best chance we can.

Unity, cohesion, intimacy, above all ease of access to Governors and staff—these are the precious qualities of smallness, and they are so important in rehabilitation. Experienced borstal Governors maintain that 300 is much too large for a borstal, and that 150 is a much better size. And if that is true for borstal, it must be equally true for a prison for adults whose personalities are already more set, and where the rehabilitative effort may have to be correspondingly greater. The pioneer Social Rehabilitation Unit[1] at Belmont run by Dr. Maxwell Jones is even smaller than 150.

But if the experiment succeeds, I fully recognize that we shall not be able to build a whole network of small new prisons.

[1] A unit, attached to a mental hospital, for patients with character abnormalities (psychopaths). Some of the patients have broken the law. The unit is run as a therapeutic community. For further information, see Maxwell Jones, *Social Psychiatry*. Tavistock Publications Ltd. 1952.

We shall largely have to adapt what we already have, and only gradually replace the old by the new. This is not only a matter of economic necessity but actually desirable.

For such a period of gradual change in classification methods, in the structure of buildings, in the prison system itself would allow the time essential for corresponding changes to take place in the organization of the Prison Service, which would also have to become a more highly trained and professional service than it is now. Reorganized, with a new structure and able to master new techniques, its task would be to exploit our growing knowledge of behaviour and of the human mind, and to bring its skill to bear, in a concerted effort, not just on a few 'abnormal' offenders but upon all those whom the courts will not allow to be dealt with in freedom.

There is more than a hint of this already in the White Paper. In the chapter on Staff and the development of new human relations, there is the following heartening passage:

'If this is to be tackled by men who have, in general, no previous qualifications or training for such work, it is necessary to give them, so far as possible, the necessary techniques. Steps have already been taken to provide training in casework for the Assistant Governor grades. New techniques such as group therapy on the medical side and group discussion on the lay side are also being developed. In this connexion, the research projects now being carried out into the structure and group reactions of the prison community are of great interest and importance. The development of techniques above mentioned must depend on a much more informed appreciation of these fundamental problems of prison management.'

21
The New Prison

ASSUMING that agreement had been reached to build one small new maximum security prison for 150 prisoners, and to begin an experiment in treatment, what sort of a building should it be, what sort of a staff would be required, what should be the régime, and what the underlying assumption which should guide treatment?

Buildings. I should like the buildings so constructed that the sleeping and living quarters of the prisoners were divided into twelve small separate units, each for twelve or thirteen prisoners. Each unit might have a small dormitory for, say, six; six single rooms or cells; one common room where all meals, including breakfast, would be taken, and which would be the place where group therapy and group discussions could be held; a bathroom and a lavatory; and a small office for the Unit or Group Officer.

I should also like to see twelve small workshops, each for twelve or thirteen prisoners; and I should want to see each group of prisoners remain a group—i.e. they would live together in one unit, and work together in one workshop.

A group of that size remaining together is not my invention, of course. It is about the size of the small therapeutic community at the psychiatric unit at Wormwood Scrubs—a promising experiment in group therapy. And it was there that it was found, by trial and error, that roughly twelve or thirteen is about the best size. And as a group, it is just small enough for every member of it still to count as an individual.

But apart from these considerations, there would be the fact that small groups are easier for officers to handle. A large workshop can be a rather threatening place, containing a lot of unknown and possibly dangerous quantities. A small workshop has in it a few people one cannot help but get to know well.

It might even be useful to have pairs of workshops, for example

2 carpenter shops
2 tailor shops
2 brush making shops
2 bookbinding shops
2 boot repair shops
2 small laundries

It does not matter what shops precisely, but apart from the possible difficulty of having twelve different small workshops, pairs of shops together with living units of equal size would open the way for controlled experiments in a manner which would not be possible otherwise. This might well become important when it comes to testing and refining treatment techniques.

Cleaning and minor repairs of each unit would be done by the unit group. Library and stores I should like to see run by officers (or perhaps by civilians) but at any rate, there ought not to be a few prisoners in specially privileged positions. The same applies to the cookhouse. Ideally, I should like to see the cooking for prisoners and single staff done by women (as is the case in many small Scandinavian prisons). There are quite a few sound psychological reasons, and sometimes perhaps also some culinary ones, why the preparation of food should be in the hands of women.

The Prison Officers Association might object to these heretical ideas. Nor would I make an issue of this small point. But why should it object? The women could be members of the Association, and the men could get on with the difficult and far more professional job of rehabilitation.

I need not emphasize why I should not want prisoners in the cookhouse, the stores, the library, or any other special and privileged position. These are some of the places where there might be a bit of fiddling and black-marketeering, and I would like to cut this down at least to some extent.

To this might be added the reasons why I do want the group to stay together:

(*a*) To be able to control the balance of personalities in each group

(*b*) To be able to influence internal leadership within the group

(*c*) Through (*a*) and (*b*), and by group discussion and group therapy, to be able to influence the climate of prisoner public opinion in each group.

Strictly speaking, these points ought really to be made under the headings *Régime* and *Treatment*, but since they are so intimately connected with the structure of the building, they must also come in here. And that brings me to a general proposition. I do not know how far the precise suggestions I am making are practical possibilities.[1] But I am convinced that the structure of a prison determines to a considerable extent the sort of human relations which go on within it. I also believe that if you really want to exercise social control over prisoners, you cannot do it adequately when there are 1,000 of them, or 500, or even 300; no matter how many rules and regulations are laid down for their conduct. You can get much nearer to it if you divide them into small groups, *and keep them divided*. Divide and conquer. These two factors should therefore be taken into account when new prisons are being planned.

I am aware of quite some uneasiness in myself as I write these lines. If small groups really would lead to staff dominance, as I believe, do I really want such dominance?

I want the possibility of such dominance. But only in some such context as that described here, and solely for the purpose of helping the twisted to straighten and the immature to grow up. For that purpose, the deliberate control and manipulation of the social and psychological forces within the small group is permissible.

---

[1] I do know of one young architect, however, who got his professional qualification by blue-printing a prison embodying these features.

It is certainly no worse than locking a large group into a large prison, and passively allowing the haphazard development of psychological and social forces to do its evil work. And that these forces do tend to be negative when they are not controlled, I hope I have shown earlier in the book. Finally, if we have a right to punish (and some would say we have a right to flog and even to hang) then I believe we have a right, and also a duty, to help prisoners to rehabilitate themselves and to try 'to establish in them', as the Statutory Rule has it, 'the will to lead a good and useful life on discharge'.

To return to the small prison: I have no special views about the administrative buildings except that I should like to see a staff conference room, either as part of the Governor's office, or next to it. There should also be somewhere about the place one large hall which could hold all prisoners and staff together.

As for the group units, each unit should be secure in itself, as should the individual cells and the dormitory within it. In addition to the group units, there would also have to be a reception unit of about the same size.

Staff. We have already in the Prison Service some Governors who have undergone a course of special training in group relations at the Tavistock Clinic; and by the time it takes to build a small prison, there should be more. One of these should be the Governor of the new prison. He would want a lot of say in what staff he would like, but this is what I would suggest to him:

2 Assistant Governors
1 Medical Officer with psychiatric training
1 Psychologist with knowledge of group therapy
1 Tutor Organizer (or Education Officer, if by then he has become a member of the Prison Service)
1 Social Worker, preferably after having undergone a generic case-work course; and preferably a woman. Her job would be case-work in connexion with ultimate release and after-care
1 Chief Officer
4 Principal Officers (3 of whom would also be in charge of three units each, and the other in charge of the reception unit)

40 Basic Grade Officers[1] (12 of whom would also be in charge of one unit each)

Régime. The prison would also have to find out how it could best go along. Basically, and especially at the beginning, the routine might be much the same as that of an ordinary prison. For the prisoners, the hours between 7 a.m. and 8.30 or 9 a.m. would be taken up by washing and shaving; having breakfast; cleaning their unit; reporting sick, etc. Then off to work, followed by exercise (where contact with other groups is inevitable); lunch; more work; tea; then leisure, evening classes, games, etc. Such, briefly, might be their day to start with.

For the Officers, however, it would be rather different already. At reception, a provisional allocation of prisoners into groups and workshops would have been made; but was it the right allocation?

While the prisoners are at work, the Group Officers would meet, with the Governor or one of the Assistant Governors, perhaps the M.O., the Social Worker, the Psychologist, and the Principal Officers concerned, to discuss the composition of their groups, and the personalities in them. This meeting would probably have to take place every day so that the right adjustments and groupings could be made. The decision to alter groups would be made in the light of everyone's experience, for everyone would begin to know everyone else's group, and therefore the weight of another fellow's problems.

Group Officer A would not want to have a more difficult group than Group Officer B. On the other hand, if Group Officer C really had an unfair proportion of tricky customers, it would only seem right to share the burden. So that, in a sense, a good number of the staff would take part in a continuous process of classification.

Yet often it might not be possible to shift the burden. Every Group Officer, every Principal Officer would have to accept his share of difficulties. But they could also share their knowledge and understanding of how to cope with them. Group Officer D would say that this is what he did in such and such a

---

[1] Allowing for a two-shift system.

situation, Group Officer E how he tackled another, and so on. People would learn from each other's mistakes as well as from each other's successes.

This would get group discussion amongst staff going. Week by week, there would be new arrivals and new departures, week by week the process of classification and adjustment would go on, and more experience would be gained in grouping and handling.

And now—and only now—the time might be ripe to move on to other things. I strongly believe that the staff ought first to be allowed to find their feet, to become familiar with group discussion, to gain confidence in this method and in themselves and to experience the feeling of mutual support which comes out of such discussions.

Already, the staff discussions would have a dynamic of their own—continuous classification and the simpler handling of problems. Now the machinery could be speeded up a little by beginning prisoner discussion. One day, one of the Assistant Governors or the Psychologist would say that he wanted to start this. Which group should he start on?

Discussion. Eventually, *the staff group as a whole* would choose a group. (Before having experience of genuine group discussions, I suspect they would have been inclined to wait to be told which group it was to be.) That afternoon, the unit group (of prisoners) has its first group discussion. The next morning, the staff group begins to digest the experience.

Gradually, all groups start discussion. They are only started by the Governor, the Assistant Governor, the Psychologist, or the M.O. What are they about? Almost anything. What am I going to do when I get out of here? How did I get here? Why do I steal? What is it like to be illegitimate? What should my girl do if she has a baby? How should I bring up children? What was my childhood like?

All these topics are important as subjects, important to the prisoners, and to those who are entrusted with their care. In discussing them, the prisoners begin to reveal themselves, not only by what they actually say, but by the way they say it, and by the way they react to each other. The masks begin to drop, it may become possible to see where their difficulties lie, and how they became as they are.

127

The aim of group discussion and group-therapy (which should only be started by personnel with special training) is to facilitate the dropping of masks, the gradual realization of what the others are really like, and what one is really like oneself.[1] The group gains insight, as a group, and each individual gains some insight into others and into himself. As he gains insight, so he can gradually learn to adopt a more realistic pose, an attitude designed to meet a particular situation with common-sense, and not with hostility, or by an attempt to evade the problem altogether. (It also sets processes in motion within the group which the group must work out itself. That is another reason why it is important to keep the prisoner group together as much as possible, working, eating, talking, laughing.)[2]

Once work is over (and I envisage group discussion or group therapy during working hours—it is the most important work which prisoners can do), the place can become a hive of leisure activity. To release all this energy, some intermingling of groups must be allowed. This is the time when they have classes, give concerts, produce plays, have competitions, follow hobbies, paint. These things will matter to them, and they should be allowed and encouraged to organize much of these activities themselves. The second shift will be on (I hope there would be a shift system for the staff), and a new lot of Officers would be with a new lot of small groups. And every now and then, the Social Worker would want to consult them about a prisoner, and his progress towards release or transfer to an open prison,

[1] Since this was written, group counselling has gradually begun in various prisons and borstals. This is a method of undirected group discussion between a member of the staff and small groups of inmates. Inmates generally tend to express hostility at first but later they will turn to genuine problems. Already it can be said that group counselling usually decreases tensions between staff and inmates, and increases mutual understanding. Group counselling may therefore make life in institutions easier for everyone—but it need not necessarily lead to the rehabilitation of more offenders. Since there is comparatively little staff training, group counsellors may not always utilize the potentialities of the group fully, or interpret to its members what goes on. But it is upon good interpretation that the growth of insight depends, and in my view, insight is an important preliminary to rehabilitation. Nevertheless, the development of group counselling must be most warmly welcomed as an important step forward, and one that should give custodial staff greater opportunities to play an important part in treatment and rehabilitation.

[2] It must be remembered, however, that every week there would be new arrivals and departures so that no groups would ever remain absolutely constant for any length of time.

the M.O. about another, the Governor might want views about the new pottery class, or about a prisoner coming up for report the following day.

But it is not really possible to write of all this as if it were some dead blue-print. I do not really know at all how it would be in practice, except that I hope that the place would be alive and humming. The Governor would put his stamp on it, staff and prisoners would come up with ideas I have not thought of at all, and I should expect the Basic Grade Officers particularly to play an important part in all this—as contributors rather than as recipients of orders from above.

The prisoners at this new prison might be men serving anything from three months to several years. But with longer sentences, the aim would be transfer to an open institution or a hostel after a suitable period of training. Very long sentence prisoners would have to be in special institutions, as would the most difficult psychopaths (who should be under medical supervision); and those who receive less than three months—a category one hopes would slowly diminish—would also have to be housed separately.

I would not expect the new methods of classification to run into any major difficulties, and I should also expect the Group Officers to get on very well with their small groups—except for one category of prisoner: the highly intelligent. Prisoners of that kind often have very real difficulties. They talk a different language, and their education, far from being a help, may cut them off from prisoners and staff. There may be a real barrier in communications, and they are often pushed into a position of false superiority, irritating to others and destructive to themselves.

I feel, therefore, that intelligence would be an important factor in grouping. It would probably be possible to have special groups, heterogeneous as far as personalities are concerned but all with a high I.Q. And for such groups, there might have to be special Group Officers, possibly even Social Workers or A.G.IIs. The problem is not an easy one at all, and I am not sure what the best answer might be.

Assumptions behind Treatment. There must always be some basic assumption behind treatment, some plan to which the whole process is geared. I do not pretend the assumptions I would make are the right ones. They are very simple, common ground amongst many who deal with delinquency, but they are not susceptible to the kind of controlled experiments which are now, rightly, becoming a must in criminology. I just have a hunch they might be right; and they lead to a treatment dynamic whereas some other assumptions one could make (which might turn out to be more accurate) do not.

I would have three broad general aims: to give prisoners and staff more insight; to provide facilities for identification by prisoners with staff (and, to a lesser extent, by staff with superior staff); and to provide opportunities for, and pressure towards, role-taking.

How have I arrived at these aims, and what do they mean? I have arrived at them by making an assumption that the one characteristic which almost all prisoners share is some degree of emotional immaturity, some childishness in the sphere of feeling.

Small children have not yet learned how to control their behaviour. They have not yet learned how to wait, to bear frustration, to do without, to consider others. They are still at the stage where they take but cannot yet give. They are unable to assess the effects of their actions, they do not yet know how to put themselves into someone else's shoes: they have still to learn role-taking (taking someone else's role).

Small children learn about behaviour from their parents, not only because parents say, do this, don't do that, but also because they want to grow to be like their parents. A little girl will watch how her mother moves and walks and talks and dresses, she models herself on Mother. She plays with her doll and pretends she *is* Mother. Children learn by identification with adults whom they love and trust. That is, if they can. But if something goes wrong with identification (illegitimacy, absence of, or rejection by, one or both of the parents), a mark is left, and the process of growing up, of maturation, is impeded. Boys need their father, particularly at certain stages; and if their father also represents authority in the family, and they cannot identify with him, then their future relationship with authority figures may turn out to be unsatisfactory.

Prisoners may be fully grown in body and in intellect but still remain immature in some of their reactions. Many of them cannot put themselves into the other fellow's shoes, for example, of the man whom they are deceiving or from whom they are stealing. And they often cannot come to terms with those in authority—first at home, then at school, then at work. Ultimately they may be at war with all who represent law and order in society.

Based on these assumptions, treatment would be so arranged that there are opportunities for developing good relations, and some identification, with authority figures. The chances of gaining insight would come mainly from group discussion and group therapy, as would the beginning of role-taking. This could be further developed in leisure activities and through certain measures of self-administration. In some respects, and on some occasions, prisoners would have to be taken through childhood experiences—stages in their early development which were missed or which had gone wrong.

None of this is in any way new or original. It has been done, and in much subtler ways than I have indicated, within a prison —but it has not been done throughout a prison. I hope it will be tried.

I also hope that one day, when we know a little more, and can perhaps be a little surer of our assumptions, someone will write a Treatment Manual[1] so that the great wealth of skill and know-how which has been, and will be, accumulated in the Prison Service can be made more widely available.

---

[1] There is already a useful pamphlet on group discussions with prisoners: 'What Will Be Your Life?' By Norman Fenton, Deputy Director of Classification and Treatment, California State Department of Corrections. Published by the American Correctional Association.

22
The Way Back

THE way back into society really starts, or should do, when an offender first arrives in prison. But however well the régime inside may be designed to help him to grow out of anti-social attitudes, the sentence itself often evokes a hostile reaction on the part of the public. Whatever may be gained by treatment and training is in danger of being lost again if society puts obstacles in the way of resettlement.

Moreover, the sudden interruption of, and withdrawal from ordinary life, the mere fact of having to live in a special community, segregated from family and the rest of the world outside, have themselves psychological and social consequences which make a smooth return to the community more difficult. Things can never be quite as they were before.

Take the hopeful case of a first offender who is lucky enough to have a home, a family, and a wife who is prepared to stand by him. However hard they both try, the relationship between husband and wife will inevitably be affected. The wife may feel pity and affection but she will not be able to feel respect. Her confidence in her husband is bound to have been shaken, her trust in him as a responsible human being, able to take care of, and protect, her and the children.

And what about the children themselves? They need to be able to model themselves on their father who is so much bigger and stronger and older and more powerful than they are, and who tells them what to do and what not to do. But how can they? The damage done to children when their father has been revealed as a criminal, has been punished, has lost his social position, perhaps his job, almost certainly his authority —this damage can be considerable. Quite apart from the shock and the loss of faith, there may be neighbours and neighbours' children to contend with, school and the merciless jibes of their classmates.

Such is the bitter irony inherent in the situation that the more insight the offender has, or gains, the more clearly will he see the difficulties that face him. The man who leaves prison dreading the things that lie before him, his confidence shattered, may need help and reassurance desperately before he can recover some place in the community again. But the man who swaggers out of the gate, sure that everything will turn out all right now that he is free at last, may need help even more, for he may be unable to assess his position realistically

That help must come in the first instance from the Social Worker in prison. A few years ago, a Departmental Committee[1] recommended that trained social workers (Prison Welfare Officers) should be appointed, one in every prison, and several in the larger ones. Their function was to undertake all the necessary case-work in connexion with preparation for release and after-care. They are now being appointed as quickly as suitable candidates become available. It may not be easy to find them, partly because there is an endemic shortage of social workers, and possibly also because many social workers may prefer the comparative freedom and recognized status of a Probation Officer to the need to build up their position within the prison and also *vis-à-vis* the local Discharged Prisoners Aid Society. This may be a real difficulty until these voluntary bodies become accustomed to the concepts and standards of proper case-work, and the much more independent status which the modern case-worker needs as compared with the old Welfare Agent who concentrated mainly on immediate financial aid on discharge.

On the other hand, there are now sound plans for building up a real prison social service, with possibly rather better opportunities for promotion than in probation. And, as the

[1] Report of the Committee on Discharged Prisoners' Aid Societies. H.M.S.O. Cmd. 8879. 1953.

service gradually establishes itself, so new traditions will begin to emerge and the conditions of this constructive and challenging work will improve.

The job of a case-worker in prison (I dislike the term Prison Welfare Officer with its aura of charity and do-gooding) can be divided into three components: case-work with the prisoner; case-work with his family (if any), or the arranging for such case-work; and a smooth link-up with whatever after-care organization will take over after release.

Case-work with the prisoner. The following is a useful definition of case-work[1]:

'. . . case-workers . . . aim at . . . changes in underlying attitudes which affect the individual's solving of his problems. This we attempt to do by mobilizing the healthy part of the personality to try to set in motion the natural healing forces present in everyone. At the same time we show the client we are aware of and accept his hostile, negative feelings without being harmed by them and, in addition, we often have to demonstrate to him how he has carried the past into the present.'

This implies an assessment of the prisoner's personality, of his chances of progress in prison, of the kind of situation he is likely to have to meet outside, and of the possibilities within him of coping with that situation. It means co-operation and consultation with those who are responsible for carrying out the general treatment programme, but it is important to stress that it does not mean usurping their functions.[2] The treatment staff must always remember the outside but concentrate on the here and now. The case-worker must bear in mind the present but should concentrate on planning for discharge and after. Or rather, she (for it may be a woman) must help the prisoner to plan. This may involve practical plans for family reconciliation (when applicable), or finding suitable lodgings and work.

Wherever this is possible and realistic, the prisoner should be encouraged to write his own letters for jobs and lodgings.

---

[1] From Lloyd Davies. *The Boundaries of Case-Work.* Association of Psychiatric Social Workers. 1956.

[2] An attempt to analyse the social worker's role *vis-à-vis* the rest of the staff was made in Chapter 10.

The case-worker may have to find out where there might be possibilities of jobs and lodging but the prisoner should always be encouraged to do as much of the preparatory work as possible—even if it only means writing letters to the probation officer in the area in which he hopes to live and work. This does not absolve the case-worker from making her own contacts and obtaining and supplying her own information. It does involve discussing and planning with the prisoner and getting him to accept some responsibility for his own future.

Case-work with the prisoner's family. This may be difficult as the prisoner and his family may be in different parts of the country. (The fact that a prisoner has constructive links in a particular area might well be one of the determinants in deciding which prison to send him to.) But even if it is not possible for the case-worker herself to visit the family at home, she should arrange for a number of interviews before or after visits, and should also have a say in the frequency of visits and letters to the prisoner, and the timing of home leave.

The problems of the family should be discussed both with the family (including, if at all possible, the children), and with the prisoner. Again, possible solutions should be discussed with all concerned, but some of the plans and their execution left to the prisoner and his family. It is important that he (and they) feel he is still able to do something for them, and this applies even if most of it has to be done by remote control, through Probation Officers or other after-care agencies.

Link-up with After-Care. This, and the after-care itself, may well turn out to be one of the most difficult tasks of all. Strictly speaking, the case-worker should link up only with the Discharged Prisoners' Aid Societies. She is, in fact, employed by the Headquarters of these voluntary societies—the National Association of Discharged Prisoners' Aid Societies. However, her work is just as important for the gradually extending number of prisoners who come under statutory after-care, and therefore under the care of Probation Officers.

Whichever agency she links up with, she should furnish it with details of the prisoner's background, personality, training progress, assessment of capabilities, family situation, etc., and she should do her planning for release and after-care with and through the agency, as well as with the prisoner himself. The kind of information which is obtained by the Borstal Division of the Central After-Care Association is a model of what is required.

Whenever possible, the person responsible for after-care, whether Probation Officer or Agent of the Discharged Prisoners' Aid Society, should make personal contact with the prisoner while he is still serving his sentence. This preliminary getting-to-know-each-other is important both to the prisoner and the after-care worker. There is little doubt that the after-care itself should also be undertaken, or at least co-ordinated, by trained case-workers.

The discharged prisoner, particularly if he is already a recidivist, and if no real effort has been made in prison to come to grips with his inner difficulties and the basic reasons for his delinquency, can present formidable difficulties in after-care. Getting a man a roof over his head and a job to do is important, but by themselves these things do not alter his personality and he may relapse precisely because his attitude has not changed.

Friendship offered by ordinary members of the public has a place in after-care, both for its own sake and because it can become a symbol of the attitude of the public. On the other hand, there may also be some danger in relying too much on members of the public unless they are known to have some experience with offenders. The Handbook of the Probation Service[1] has some excellent passages on some of these difficulties:

'The recidivist knows well how to employ the kind of emotional blackmail implied in the phrases, "Nobody helped me", "They gave me ten shillings and turned me out", and "I lost my job when they found where I came from". Consciously or unconsciously, he will attempt to exploit the law-abiding citizen's confused feelings of guilt, responsibility and compassion, and his demands may be reinforced by fear and the desire to get even with society.'

[1] *The Probation Service.* Edited on behalf of the National Association of Probation Officers by J. F. S. King. Butterworth. 1958.

And later

'It must be realized that in most cases the prisoner's previous experience of personal relationship will in most cases have been unsatisfactory, possibly wounding and rejecting to a degree. He will not find it easy to trust anyone, and will demand tangible proofs of friendship and the desire to help. This can create a difficult situation for the case-worker. The need for material help may be a very real one, especially in dealing with the homeless, *yet help must not be given in such a way as to increase the recipient's sense of dependence and lack of worth*.' [My italics.]

It is because the private citizen or the untrained Welfare Agent may often find it hard to deal with his own feelings of guilt—which can quickly change to hostility if the prisoner does not behave according to expectations—and because he tends to rely too much on helping the prisoner and not enough on getting him to help himself, that after-care is best under-taken by trained case-workers. Private and voluntary help might best be deployed through a case-worker who, knowing both the volunteer and the prisoner, can give the former a task in which he can hope to have some success and make a real contribution.

There are a few outstanding people, in all walks of life, who are not trained but to whom these remarks do not apply. Such people have a rare gift, and whoever comes into contact with them, is enriched. But what can be expected of the ordinary, busy, pre-occupied person must not be assessed in terms of the achievements of these exceptional men and women.

Finally, one more passage from the Handbook of the Probation Service which sums up the problems of after-care in a realistic fashion:

'Many ex-prisoners, both men and women, in spite of all efforts to help them, drift endlessly between lodging-houses, hostels and furnished rooms, with intervals in prison, forming the hard core of recidivists, not only with no desire but apparently no knowledge of living any other way. This attitude the officer responsible for after-care has to try to combat, without false illusions but without despair, even in the face of the knowledge that to many of his charges prison is . . . an escape from the constant demands of society which his inadequate personality cannot or will not meet.'

After-care has often been criticized—perhaps because it is at this stage that failure becomes most obvious, irrespective of whether it lies in the help provided or in the personality of the offender. Perhaps, too, those to whom after-care is entrusted have sometimes had to bear an unfair share in the burden of rehabilitation. But, as has already been emphasized, treatment in prison and after-care are part of the same process. Improvements in the former should make the path less stony for the latter.

Whether any of the ideas—and, I daresay, prejudices—that I have briefly aired will lead to progress and better results, I do not know. I hope so. But knowing the idealism, the patience, the skill, and the humility with which some of the men and women in the Prison Service and in After-Care tackle their job, I am quite certain that progress will come.

Appendices
Introductory Note:
THE FUNCTIONS AND DUTIES
OF PRISON STAFF

IT may be useful to have an assessment of the present functions and duties of various members of the Prison Service, as they themselves see it, and as opposed to their possible attitudes and feelings and to their future role, as I see it.

By kind permission of the Prison Officers Association and of the Society of Civil Servants, the following extracts regarding these functions and duties, from the evidence offered to the Wynn-Parry Committee, are therefore reprinted.

It is only fair to recall that the Wynn-Parry Committee was set up to inquire into pay and conditions in the Prison Service. This has naturally determined the contents of the evidence given. More emphasis may have been put on the detailed description of various duties (not all of which necessarily have to be performed on the same day) than to drawing attention to, let us say, the retirement provisions which, in my opinion, are rather good.

Above all, a cold catalogue of duties does not reflect the warmth and the devotion which is often brought to the job, nor does it indicate the satisfaction which can be found in it, particularly in certain institutions. Nevertheless, I feel it is important that, in a book such as this, members of the Prison Service should be allowed at least to give a factual description of their own job.

Appendix A
THE CHANGING FUNCTIONS OF PRISON OFFICERS[1]

THE changes of the last thirty-five years have meant a complete alteration in the personal relationships between prisoners and staff and in the function which the staff is expected to perform. As long ago as 1919 the term 'Prison Officer' was substituted for the old designation 'Warder' and . . . the emphasis began from the early nineteen-twenties to be put upon the training and rehabilitation which the officer could encourage, as opposed to the purely custodial and security duties which until then made up the whole of prison work. The developments since then have, of course, carried this tendency very much farther, and while in some establishments the security and custodial duties still have considerable significance, in all prisons the emphasis is mainly and, in some cases wholly, upon the example which an officer can set and the personal influence which he can exercise over the prisoners. Nobody, moreover, can believe—or would desire to believe—that development and experiment in the prison administration have now come to an end. Along whatever precise lines the process may continue in the future, there can be little doubt that an ever-increasing importance will be put on the personal relationship between the prisoner and the staff, and that more and more will be expected of the Prison Officer.

[1] From the Memorandum of Evidence by the Prison Officers Association.

Appendix B

SOME DUTIES AND
RESPONSIBILITIES OF THE
BASIC GRADE PRISON OFFICER[1]

THE average day in the Prison Officer's life involves him commencing duty, if he is on the early shift at 7.00 a.m., which means that in order to be properly groomed for parade he has to be out of bed about 6.00 a.m. On reaching his post, his first task is to check the number of prisoners on the particular landing over which he is given control, and having done this he signs a certificate as to the number. He next unlocks his prisoners, and receives from them any applications—such as applications to see the Doctor, Chaplain, the Governor, letters, visits, etc. He tabulates these applications and then remains in immediate control during a very unpleasant period whilst the prisoners are engaged in performing their natural functions.

All meals are served on the cafeteria system and after supervising the serving of the breakfast meal and certifying the numbers locked up on his landing, the officer is now free to have his own meal. One Discipline Officer is always left in the Hall whilst the men are having their breakfast.

After breakfast, the prisoners, who have been locked up in their cells, are unlocked, and those who were received the previous night are taken away for interview by the Reception Board. The Discipline Officer is responsible to see that the appropriate records are produced to the Board and he remains with the prisoners whilst they are being interviewed. Meanwhile others of his colleagues are searching cells for signs of tampering and contraband, and to ensure that the cells are clean and tidy.

[1] From the Memorandum of Evidence by the Prison Officers Association.

The officers engaged in maintaining discipline in the workshop must be prepared for any emergency, and particularly must be on the alert in circumstances where men of violent disposition handle knives and other dangerous weapons in the course of their work. It is by no means uncommon for an officer in a workshop to have more than 100 prisoners under his control, and it will be apparent that the utmost tact and discretion are necessary to avoid serious trouble arising from time to time. During the working day prisoners are constantly being brought in and taken out of the workshop and the officer is held responsible for ensuring that at all times the number of men under his immediate control is correct.

At the end of the morning and afternoon sessions all tools in the workshop have to be checked, and an officer is not allowed to leave the prison until every tool has been accounted for. Occasionally a prisoner, as an act of spitefulness against an officer, will deliberately hide a tool in order to embarrass him, and when this occurs the whole working party may have to be searched. Occasionally also a prisoner may mutilate or destroy work or material, and the officer is held responsible for endeavouring to prevent this.

Other officers during the morning are engaged with various parties including cleaning parties, outside working parties. Other officers may be preparing records for the many and various Boards that are held, or checking or censoring incoming and outgoing letters of prisoners, or receiving incoming property and money and ensuring that it reaches the appropriate department.

At midday the prisoners are marched into their halls for dinner. The officer is responsible for ensuring that each prisoner receives his allotted meal.

After dinner work is resumed in the shops under the charge of some officer whilst other officers are required to supervise the conversations between visitors and prisoners. The regulations provide that prisoners are not allowed to talk about prison matters and that they must converse in English. An officer may be in charge of as many as eighteen Visiting Boxes with a prisoner in each, and it is clear that he has to exercise a good deal of discretion and cannot possibly ensure that the regulations are literally interpreted. At open visits—that is visits without any barrier between the prisoner and his friends—the officer is expected to see that nothing passes between the prisoner and his friends, that the visit terminates at the correct time, and he is responsible for endorsing the visiting permit.

At the conclusion of the afternoon labour period the number of prisoners are checked and unless the numbers prove correct, no officer is allowed to leave the prison. Those officers who are required for evening duty are allowed half an hour for tea, whilst the remainder leave duty normally at 5.30 p.m., having been in the prison from 7.00 a.m.

The evening routine in prisons commences by the checking of the numbers in the various halls at 5.30 p.m. After this meal, the evening duty officer, assisted by those officers detailed for the supervision of Evening Classes unlock and assemble prisoners for classes and conduct prisoners to their appropriate class at the appropriate time. During the remainder of the time the officer remains on duty, he must maintain a general over-sight of all that is going on in his Hall, must respond to all calls from prisoners in their cells and must supervise the visits paid by social workers to the prisoners, ensuring that nothing irregular takes place and that the prisoner is safely locked up after the social worker has left his cell.

The above description of the day-to-day duties of a Prison Officer has not taken account of certain special functions which all officers are liable, in turn, to perform. These include reception duties, escort and court duties and duties in the condemned cell. The officers in charge of reception are responsible that the right men are being received in accordance with the committal warrants, and that the property in the possession of a prisoner upon his admission in custody is correctly recorded and placed in safe custody. The responsibility includes also the taking of finger prints, and ensuring that these are correctly dealt with. It is of the utmost importance that strict accuracy should prevail, for it is upon these finger prints that the official record of a man's past may depend. Officers are often required to give sworn testimony in the Courts on these matters. The reception officers are responsible for compiling records and for carrying out the very distasteful task of searching prisoners

143

clothing which may be verminous or which may be taken from prisoners suffering from venereal disease, tuberculosis, skin disease, etc. Reception officers are also responsible for ensuring that a prisoner is of good appearance when he is discharged from prison.

Since the war the work of the Prison Officer has been almost completely changed. He is now required to enter into a much closer relationship with prisoners than was permitted in the past. He is required to report from time to time on the men with whom he comes in contact and is expected by his bearing and example to inculcate in them the desire to adopt a way of life which will enable them to become responsible members of the society in which they live.

Appendix C
SOME DUTIES AND
RESPONSIBILITIES OF THE
PRINCIPAL OFFICER[1]

THE Principal Officer is the first rank above the basic grade of officer, and is not reached until an average nineteen years has been served. Providing the candidate has passed the promotion examination held under the supervision of the Civil Service Commissioners, and subject to good conduct and efficiency, consideration for promotion comes when the officer enters the seniority 'field'.

A Principal Officer's duties are in the main supervisory and administrative, but as he is the disciplinary head of the Hall in which the inmates live he has a large measure of personal contact with them. His duties can be divided into four main categories and although they may differ slightly according to the type or size of the prison at which he serves, they are broadly speaking of the same responsibility throughout the service.

(a) Principal Officers are in charge of a Hall or Wing of a prison with a population ranging from 100 inmates to over 300. For example halls at Wormwood Scrubs hold over 300, whereas in a smaller type of prison, the Hall numbers would be the lower figure.

The Principal Officer supervises the officers allocated to his hall and details them for their various duties. In those prisons where there is a centre with wings leading off it, a Principal Officer is in charge of the Centre, a job which involves controlling, co-ordinating the staff activities, movement and routine of the whole prison.

[1] From the Memorandum of Evidence by the Prison Officers Association.

The Hall or Wing Principal Officer is responsible for the cleanliness generally of his Hall or Wing, with particular emphasis on the inmates' cells and toilets and dining arrangements, and for the inmates themselves and their clothing and bedding. He is responsible for the upkeep of the inmates' records, for dealing with applications for outgoing letters, and for recording incoming ones. He advises inmates on their applications to the Governor, Visiting Magistrates, and the Visiting Commissioner, and the procedure in connexion with appeals against conviction or sentence, and petitions to the Home Secretary. He also deals with complaints made by inmates and in many cases he is approached by inmates with requests for advice on domestic problems. In the larger prisons he is responsible for his own Hall canteen, and for a stock of between £80 to £100. He also pays out all the inmates in his Hall once a week. He ensures that newcomers to his Hall understand the appeal rules, and instructs them in the routine of the prison and the standard of behaviour and cleanliness required of them. He has to satisfy himself that any inmates in his Hall who are sick in their cell are properly attended to and also he may have inmates on punishment in his charge who have to be specially supervised. Routine items, such as examination of cells for security, upkeep of clothing record cards, periodical searching of inmates and their cells, drawing of stores and stationery, are all his responsibility. In addition he may have posted with him in his Hall probationary officers under training, to whom he has to give special attention with a view to teaching them their duties and reporting on them as to their suitability for establishment. Auxiliary Officers under training prior to proceeding to the Training School at Wakefield also receive part of their instruction in the Halls. The system is that one Principal Officer is in charge of their training programme at their initial establishment but this also means, in practice, the Auxiliary Officer will at various times come under the instruction of all the Principal Officers in the prison and all have to report as to their suitability for further training at the Wakefield School. The Principal Officer in the evenings takes his turn in supervising the class and association activities in the prison as a whole.

(b) When the Chief Officer is on leave or absent through sickness, the senior Principal Officer takes over his duties. This occurs more often in the smaller prisons where there is only one Chief Officer because, in addition, at the small prison the Chief Officer is often required to 'act up' for the Governor. In the larger prisons the Principal Officer takes over the duties of the Chief Officer, Class II, when the Chief Officer, Class II, takes over the duties of the Chief Officer, Class I.

(c) In the larger prisons the duties of the Orderly Officer are carried by the Principal Officers. This means that he is in charge of a prison ranging in population from perhaps 700 to 1,400 from the time that the main staff go off duty in the late afternoon until they come on duty the next day. He supervises a staff of evening duty officers until 9.00 p.m. and from then on the Night Patrol Staff. He has charge of the officers detailed to sleep in the prison to be available in case an emergency arises, such as an escape, suicide, smashing up of his cell by an inmate, and to assist in quelling any disturbance. The Orderly Officer deals with fines, bails or special releases during his tour of duty. He is responsible that the duties of all staff are carried out correctly, he must make frequent tours of inspection, and ensure that the security arrangements for the night are completed. He has to check all the keys and lock up the prison before going to bed about midnight and he is then liable to be called up during the night for any of the contingencies already mentioned and to attend to inmates requiring medical attention. He gets up before 5.00 a.m. and unlocks the cooks and takes them to the kitchen. He then makes tours of inspection of the Halls, Hospital and the grounds. He hands over prison to the Chief Officer when the main staff come on duty in the morning, filling the appropriate forms certifying the roll, state of security and the diets.

(d) In provincial local prisons and Brixton Prison in the London area, Principal Officers take charge of Courts of Assize and Sessions, and Appeal Courts. This involves being on duty from the early morning until late at night until the Assizes or Sessions are finished. These courts are almost continuous in the London area. Others vary from a few days to weeks depending on the size of the Calendar. Long distances have to be covered with large bodies of inmates. For example, Exeter Prison covers the whole of the West Country, Durham the North-East, Liverpool the North-West. In the Midlands, Birmingham is the chief centre of this work, but many other smaller prisons in all these districts share in this work. Brixton Prison covers a large portion of the Home Counties as well as the London Area.

The Principal Officer must check the Court Calendar for the Assize or Sessions and ascertain which prisoners are in custody or on bail. For those prisoners in custody his duty is to see that they are produced in Court at the time that they are required. In the London area some of the prisoners are not in his own prison. For example prisoners under twenty-one years of age, awaiting trial or sentence, are held at Wormwood Scrubs. Those over twenty-one are held at Brixton. The Principal Officer must check all records, property, private cash, earnings in prison, descriptive forms, lists of previous convictions, corrective training and preventive detention reports, warrants, and any statements required by the Court in respect of certain prisoners. He arranges for sufficient rations and cooking facilities at the Court for the prisoners, and he arranges for transport to and from the Court.

In many cases in the provinces, escorts are on the way to Court by 7.00 a.m. having collected the prisoners and breakfasted them. On arrival at the Court the Principal Officer will allot staff to their duties. He reports to the Clerk of the Court when he arrives and again checks to ensure that he has produced all the prisoners that the Court requires for the day. He also has ready the necessary reports, statements or any other matter that the Court may require. He will arrange for visits by Counsel or solicitors who wish to interview their clients, and also prisoners' relations and friends. The smooth running of a Court depends on the good relations and co-operation between the officials of the Court and the prison officials behind the scenes. For all this the Principal Officer bears the responsibility. At the end of the day he is responsible for arrangements to deliver to the appropriate prisons all prisoners convicted that day, take back to his own prison those not dealt with, and go all through the procedure again of making arrangements for the next day. During the day he may have had to discharge prisoners released by the Court. In these cases, in addition to ensuring that the man has had returned any property, private cash, money that he has earned in prison, he has to see that the man has the means to reach his home, or, if not, provide him with cash from official funds or with railway warrants or bus fares. He also issues the man with National Assistance forms. During all his duties, the Principal Officer will have in his care prisoners charged with minor offences and also those charged with more serious offences. He must take care to see that the various classifications of prisoners are observed, i.e. he must keep first offenders separate from persistent offenders, young from old, men from women, etc.

Other duties include running the prisoners earnings' scheme and main canteen in the larger prisons, the charge of large bodies of prisoners being escorted to other establishments or courts. At large prisons, Principal Officers are in charge of the main gate and the reception block. Principal Officers are selected as tutors at the Wakefield Training establishment and in this capacity they instruct new entrants to the Prison Service. More recently, the advent of the five-day week for clerical staff has meant that essential clerical and administrative work has, on Saturday morning, to be performed by members of the Principal Officer grade.

Appendix D

SOME DUTIES AND
RESPONSIBILITIES OF THE
CHIEF OFFICER[1]

EXTRACT from Standing Orders.

S.O. 625 (1) The Chief Officer is the head of the uniform staff at all times, subject to the Governor's control. In the absence of the Governor and Deputy Governor he has charge of the whole establishment and is responsible for it.

(2) He shall not be absent from the Prison more often than is absolutely necessary.

(3) He will open the prison every morning for the parade of officers.

(4) He will himself detail all discipline officers for their duties and will satisfy himself that the duties are properly carried out including the daily inspection of all cells by the Principal Officers or other officers in charge of Halls.

(5) (a) He will keep a daily report book and submit it every morning to the Governor.
(b) He will daily submit to the Governor a list of prisoners confined to cell, excluding hospital cases, and those specially located under Order 401 (1).

(6) He will keep a record of the location of every prisoner.

(7) Any order duly signed for the admission of

[1] From the Memorandum of Evidence by the Prison Officers Association.

150

persons to a prison will be produced to him and returned by him to the Governor's Office after the visitor has left. He will see that visits to prisoners take place under proper conditions.

(8) He will specially attend to the carrying out of the Governor's orders as to punishments to be inflicted on prisoners, and see that those undergoing punishment have opportunities for taking such exercise as the orders prescribe.

(9) He will see that prisoners confined under report or under punishment are provided with all the articles to which they are entitled.

(10) He will, when prisoners go out and return from labour, receive from the officers in charge of parties and check the number of prisoners in each party.

(11) He will daily, and as often as may be ordered. visit every party of prisoners while at work, both inside and outside the prison, and see that discipline and order are maintained among them, and report thereon as may be directed to the Governor.

(12) He will inspect daily such parts of the prison as may be deputed to him for inspection by the Governor under Order 552 (2) and pay frequent visits to all workshops and working parties.
Note:—Order 552 (2) relates to the duty of a Governor to depute a part of inspection to the Chief Officer when he himself is unable to carry out an inspection.

(13) He will lose no time in communicating to the Governor every circumstance which may come to his knowledge likely to affect the safety, health or comfort of the prisoners, the efficiency of the officers, or any other matter requiring the Governor's attention.

(14) He will carry out any duties that may be specially assigned to him by the Governor.

(15) He will every day receive from the Ward Officers the diet requisitions for the rations required for prisoners on the following day and after checking same deliver them with a summary thereof to the Governor.

(16) He will send to the Governor demands on the Steward for such stores, etc., as may be necessary, and no more, and report any irregularity in respect of the articles supplied in pursuance thereof.

(17) He will return to the Steward in due course all articles that are worn out.

(18) He will require all officers to prevent any waste of water, gas or electricity.

(19) He will communicate to all subordinate officers every order entered in the Governor's Order Book.

(20) On the completion of the course of instruction and of the period of first or special probation of a subordinate officer he will report upon such officer's qualifications.

(21) He, or in his absence the next senior officer, will every evening inspect the officers for night duty, and see that they are in all respects fit for duty, and fully acquainted with their duties.

(22) He will check the keys in the custody of the Gatekeeper as directed in Order 536, i.e. every day (1) on the opening of the prison, (2) when the day officers go off duty, and (3) when the prison is locked up for the night.

S.O. 626 The entries in the Chief Officer's daily report book will be the following:

The actual hours prisoners (a) go to labour, (b) return from labour, (c) go to exercise, (d) return from exercise.

What parts of the prison are searched and names of officers detailed for the purpose.

Names of officers deputed daily to take ordinary visits.

Particulars of any special visit held and the names of the officers detailed to supervise it.

Particulars of escorts dispatched and by whom inspected.

Hours of opening and final closing of the prison and checking of the keys.

Any unusual and important occurrence.

The foregoing are the official duties of a Chief Officer as defined in the Standing Order Book. But one must add to these a multitude of responsibilities that are never mentioned in print. His memory of official circulars and memoranda is accepted almost without question. At one time or another he will be called upon to explain them to new entrants to the Service who may be officers or Assistant Governors. It is his duty to ensure that mistakes are prevented and to stand by as the mentor and prompter when the new entrant is feeling his way. Most Governors will . . . admit that without the help of their Chief Officers at the start of their careers they would have found life very difficult indeed.

The Chief Officer is recognized as the 'go between' who takes the first pressure of problems that confront any Governor in his relations with a staff. Many a problem is settled in the Chief Officer's office.

Officers will often bring prisoners' problems to the Chief Officer on behalf of prisoners since he is always approachable. Because of this approachability, the Chief Officer is able to keep his finger on the pulse of the prison. The censor officer will draw the attention of the Chief Officer to any sign of a rift in a prisoner's domestic affairs that can be gleaned from an incoming letter. The Chief Officer can then give directions to help the prisoner on a major problem that might affect the discipline of a shop or landing.

It is often the case that officers turn to the Chief Officer in times of domestic distress. A kindly word in such cases can do much to keep harmony in the Staff and in the establishment. It is often the case that Chief Officers have so arranged an officer's duty as to assist him to overcome problems at home.

The Chief Officer will deputize for his Governor and often he will be 'acting up' to the rank above for as much as four months in each year. He will take applications, deal with infringements against discipline and will be making decisions hourly. He is held responsible for the discharge of prisoners at the proper time. In doing so he must see that they are properly dressed, supplied with the clothing necessary for the prevailing weather conditions, that they are supplied with the money or warrants to get them home, and to be able to advise them upon their future. When inmates are to be sent to court it is his responsibility to see that the escorts are sufficiently manned having due regard to the quality, quantity, and characters of the inmates concerned. Here again he must ensure that they are properly dressed so that they are dressed in a seemly condition when they appear before the court. He will at week-ends have to arrange transport for escorts. The advent of the five-day week has thrown an additional burden upon Chief Officers when dealing with the receptions of Friday and Saturday. Writing up reports to courts, booking particulars of the antecedents of remands and arranging that the courts are supplied with adequate reports.

As a result of recent instructions he is now held responsible for the control of floating stock, furniture, clothing, and kindred equipment. The control of labour so that it is used to the best advantage is also laid at his door.

If there is a query about the messing accounts he is expected to provide the answer. The uniform of his officers must be inspected by him and misuse of the Commissioners' property is investigated under his control.

The training of young entrants is also part of his responsibility. It is his duty to keep a paternal eye upon the progress of these officers through all the stages of their pre-Wakefield training and to maintain the requisite close control upon them when they are posted from Wakefield. Advice that is incorrect at this stage can have far-reaching effects later in the Officer's career.

The example set by a Chief Officer filters down through all

grades of a staff. The ideal Chief Officer must combine patience with tact. He must appear calm in even the most disturbing situations and he must react quickly in any given situation. He must inspire confidence in his Staff and he must handle both staff and prisoners with firmness and determination. He must be impartial and at no time give cause for any suggestion of favouritism.

Appendix E

SOME DUTIES AND
RESPONSIBILITIES OF GOVERNORS
AND ASSISTANT GOVERNORS[1]

THE Governor is ultimately responsible to the Prison Commissioners not only for the good order and discipline of the prison, but for every aspect of its administration and management. The requirements of the job might be stated as follows:

(a) Leadership of a large staff of professional and non-professional workers. It is the Governor who will set the tone of the establishment because the staff will always take their lead from him. Many of the staff are people with great experience in this work but there are, at the same time, young, keen, enthusiastic Assistant Governors and Officers to whom the Governor has a major responsibility, because the training they get from him is going to affect the future of the Prison Service.

(b) Leadership of prisoners. The Governor occupies what might be called an unnatural position in the prison because there is an army of officials between him and the prisoners. If his prison is going to be any use he has got to break through this barrier and get to know the prisoners personally, and a certain amount of the Governor's time must be spent in personal and private interviews with men, especially those serving long sentences. Any prisoner can ask to see the Governor any day concerning any matter he chooses and the Governor is bound to see him himself. Much of this

---

[1] From the Memorandum of Evidence by the Society of Civil Servants.

156

work is delegated to Assistant Governors but there are always a number of men who will only talk to the Governor himself and they are invariably the most difficult cases.

(c) The Governor is responsible today for a great amount of propaganda. This may take two forms:

  (i) Taking parties or individuals from all over the world round the prison on Home Office orders. All these wish to see the Governor personally and to discuss their own particular problems with him.

  (ii) Speaking at public meetings. Only by doing this can public opinion be influenced to support the work of rehabilitation that has been done in the prisons.

(d) The Governor is responsible for the physical maintenance of the establishment. Many prisons are old and the maintenance of the fabric needs constant watching. This is done by the Works Department of the prison which is also responsible for the maintenance of a large amount of valuable modern machinery in the workshops. In addition, there are Officers' Quarters that have to be kept in order. The Governor has got to keep his eye on all these points unless his establishment is going to deteriorate.

(e) He is responsible for the work done in the prison. There are workshops consisting of a variety of trades which have to be staffed by prisoners. In addition, there are Vocational Training classes and various domestic parties, e.g. parties working on sites outside the prisons. All these need supervision so that production and training can be maintained at maximum efficiency.

(f) The Governor is the sub-accounting officer. He is responsible, too, for the maintenance of approved standards of food, clothing and the application of earnings schemes. He is Chairman of the 'Consultative Committee' at his establishment, a committee representing all grades of staff to discuss policy and general administration. He attends or is represented at Inmate

Participation Councils. In accordance with Whitley procedure, he meets committees or representatives of local branches of Staff Associations.

(g) Education and social activities. Especially in a prison containing men serving very long sentences, the Governor is responsible for seeing that the men are kept mentally alive. To ensure this he must see that he has a large active educational system, an up-to-date modern library and active voluntary Prison Visitors, and if the work of the Prison Visitors is to be of value, it is essential that the Governor should make regular personal contact with them. This, of course, can usually be done only in the evenings.

(h) After-care. The Governor is a member of the various after-care committees, and he is frequently invited to give his opinion as to the best method of helping men on discharge. Long before that, however, the Governor has usually been instrumental in putting into motion on the day of reception, machinery which will ensure that the man's home and family are looked after while he is in custody.

(i) Family interviews. The Governor receives many requests for personal interviews regarding the prisoners from wives, husbands, parents and children. These requests must be granted and each family has its own particular problems.

In addition to the general supervisory functions which he discharges, his most important daily statutory duties are:—

(i) To visit and inspect daily all parts of the prison where prisoners are working or accommodated;

(ii) To see and give special attention to every prisoner who is a hospital patient;

(iii) To visit all prisoners under punishment;

(iv) To hear the applications of all prisoners who apply to see him;

(v) To investigate all offences against discipline.

Assistant Governors Class I are usually Deputy Governors in prisons or in charge of separate camps. They are required to assist the Governor in the performance of his duties and to deputize for him in his absence. Their responsibilities may include the allocation of prisoners' work; supervision of vocational and industrial training; interviewing and reporting upon Auxiliary Officers under training; and sitting on the Selection Board for officer candidates. They are usually responsible for Civil Defence training at their establishments; they supervise the prisoners' earnings schemes, check orders of court and committals, and release dates. They attend and often are in charge of Reception Boards interviewing new prisoners.

Assistant Governors Class II may act as housemasters or housemistresses in borstals or be in charge of groups of prisoners. They may be directly responsible for a Hall comprising about 100 prisoners or more to whom they act in the capacity of housemaster or housemistress. All members of the Governor Class are required to establish and maintain personal contact with the prisoners under their charge, to train and develop their characters, to supervise their vocational training, their education and recreation, to be responsible for their physical well-being and generally to assist in inculcating in them 'the will to lead a good and useful life of discharge'. The closest contact in all these respects is maintained by the Assistant Governor Class II. The borstal housemaster or housemistress has the care of young persons under the age of twenty-one. He has to win their respect and confidence and on his example and leadership may depend whether a young life is turned from the path of crime to that of useful citizenship.

Some Books

dealing with Human Groups, Group Therapy,
and Human Relations in Prison

Clemmer, Donald *The Prison Community.*
        The Christopher Publishing House, 1940.
        (Re-issued 1957)

Foulkes, S. H., and *Group Psychotherapy.*
Anthony, E. J.   Pelican, 1958.

Homans, C.   *The Human Group.*
        Routledge & Kegan Paul, 1951.

Klein, J.   *The Study of Groups.*
        Routledge & Kegan Paul, 1956.

Sprott, W. J. H. *Human Groups.*
        Pelican, 1958.

Sykes, G. M.   *The Society of Captives.*
        Princeton University Press, 1958.